Joan Wulff's **FLY-CASTING ACCURACY**

BOOKS BY *Joan Wulff*

Joan Wulff's Fly-Casting Techniques

*Joan Wulff's Fly Fishing: Expert Advice
from a Woman's Perspective*

Joan Wulff's Fly-Casting Accuracy

Joan Wulff's
FLY-CASTING ACCURACY

THE LYONS PRESS

Printed in the United States of America

10 9 8 7 6 5 4 3 2 1

Design by Cindy LaBreacht

Library of Congress Cataloging-in-Publication Data

Wulff, Joan.
    [Fly-casting accuracy]
    Joan Wulff's fly-casting accuracy.
      p.   cm.
    ISBN 1-55821-484-4.—ISBN 1-55821-465-8 (pbk.)
    1. Fly casting.   I. Title.
  SH454.2.W83   1997
  799.1'24—dc21   97-42412
                               CIP

The portion of Glenn Law's 1983 *Fly Rod & Reel* article is used herein with his kind permission.

CONTENTS

Introduction 7

1 The Elements of Accuracy 11

2 Behind the Rod 17

3 The Stroke 25

4 Looking at Accuracy in Slow Motion 35

5 Putting It All Together: Pickup, False Casting,
Hovering, and Tension 45

6 Accuracy in All Planes, Forehand and Backhand 51

7 Shooting Line and Double Hauling 55

8 Lining Up 65

9 The Roll Cast 73

10 Accuracy under Fishing Conditions 77

11 Indoor and Outdoor Practice 85

12 Strengthening Your Casting Muscles 89

Checklist 95

Introduction

If you've been fishing for any length of time you've undoubtedly heard of the angler's three stages of development: most fish, biggest fish, most difficult fish. For those of us who have spent a lifetime with fly rod in hand there is a fourth stage—a feeling of coming home, of happiness just to *be there* in the beautiful places and clean water where gamefish thrive. Personal success becomes secondary to sharing the experience with a family member or friend.

Fly casting has its own developmental stages: The beginning fly caster is delighted when line and leader fall to the water without tangling and the cast is reasonably accurate. Next comes the quest for distance. Distance is so satisfying; it's a wonderful feeling to watch the extension of your effort, a fly-line loop moving away from you at high speed, unrolling "out where the big ones are." Even though most fish are hooked at less than 50 feet, distance tends to be the standard by which premier casters are judged. My own reputation as a caster hinges on two events: I once won a national distance event against all-male competition, and I have cast a fly 161 feet.

Unfortunately, many anglers never progress beyond casting as far as they can and therefore miss the third stage: executing each cast, short or long, with grace and precision. With this comes a new joy. Every move counts; there is no wasted effort. Not only are you accurate on both short and long targets but you also accomplish accuracy with a minimum number of casting strokes. You know how to do it!

Doing something extremely well has its own rewards. If you take pride in doing anything that requires skill and discipline, you will love this third stage. If you aren't a disciplinarian it's my job to pique your interest and provide the essential elements with which you can improve your accuracy in spite of yourself.

The Nature of Fly Casting

In spinning or baitcasting, the heavy lures can be thrown by hand almost as far as they can be cast; it's like throwing a rock with a string trailing behind it.

Fly fishers' lures are imitations of essentially weightless insects constructed of fur, feathers, tinsel, and yarn. If we were to attempt to throw a sample of any of those materials—a feather, for instance—it would fall at our feet or be taken by the wind.

The weight we cast is in the fly line itself. It is flexible weight; you can cast a fly line by hand, without using a rod. The fly goes along merely as a passenger, and the heavier the fly, the harder it is to cast.

The form of the cast is an open-ended unrolling loop, and this loop must be created and unrolled in *two* directions. This makes fly casting different from all other sports. One stroke is sufficient for tennis, golf, baseball, or badminton, where you set up slowly on the backswing and knock the heck out of something on the forward stroke. Fly casters need *two* strokes: one to unroll the line behind us (a **backcast** stroke), and one to unroll the line ahead of us (the **forward cast** stroke). Therein lies the initial challenge: We don't have muscles in place trained to throw backward!

Training is the solution to efficient fly casting. Only through conscious thought and repetition do our muscles learn their jobs. The combination of mental focus and the physical effort of throwing backward, repeated a hundred times, should give you a good start.

Figure 1: The nature of fly casting: open-ended loops that unroll opposite each other.

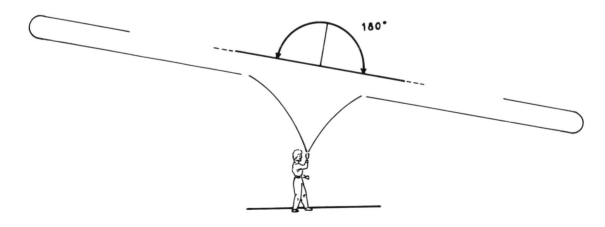

180°

Additional practice occurs naturally when you fish. Each full cast contains a backward stroke, unrolling *opposite* the forward stroke. Although you can often get by with a sloppy backcast in easy conditions (no backwind or obstacles), to be a good caster *you must know* exactly where your backcast is unrolling.

In golf and tennis instruction, players are told to visualize their shots before making them. Good casters also visualize the path of both backcast and forward cast relative to the target area before making the first move to take line off the water.

CHAPTER 1

The Elements of Accuracy

The first essential element of accuracy is coordination between your eyes and the rod hand, relative to a target. **Eye/hand/target.** It's a natural coordination: Every time you throw a used towel into a hamper or a crumpled paper into the wastebasket you're putting it to use. Its components are *alignment*, *trajectory* (relative to the distance), and *force* (relative to the weight of the object). The act of accurately casting a fly contains the same elements.

Throwing paper into a wastebasket requires either a perfectly straight line between your hand and the wastebasket or an arc for trajectory. Your hand produces an arc by throwing on a *straight line* at a chosen angle (see figure 2). In casting, movement of the rod shaft on a *straight hand/target line* takes care of that angle and determines the arc through which the rod tip moves. In turn, that arc produces the desired trajectory of the fly-line loop. This is not complicated; it's simple. Instead of computing the number of inches the arc should contain you need only think about moving your rod hand along a straight line.

In your present surroundings, choose a target 15 to 20 feet away—a chair, perhaps. When you look at the chair as a whole, an imaginary line stretches between your eyes and the chair. This is an **eye/target line.**

1. Hold your primary hand vertically with fingers extended upright, and position it close to your head so that your thumbnail is an inch higher than directly between your eyes. Pretend you're thumbing your nose—at forehead level. Don't bend your wrist backward. Look at the angle between your forearm and upper arm. It should be roughly 90 degrees.

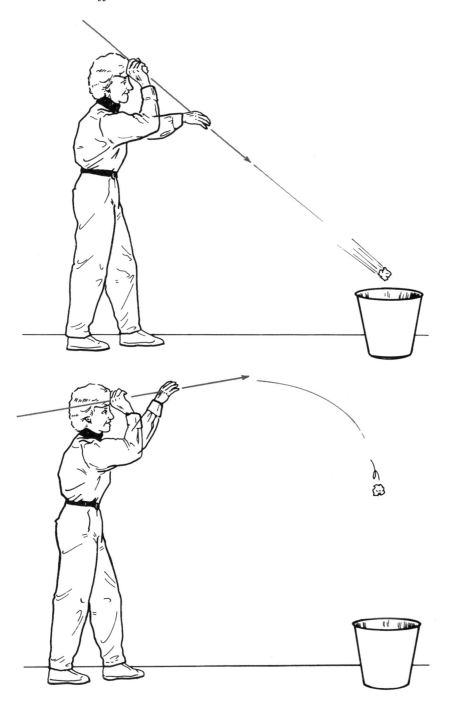

Figure 2: Throw straight at a chosen angle (top); throw straight to the apex of an arc (bottom).

You've created a second imaginary line, the one between your hand and the target—the **hand/target line.** These two imaginary lines, eye/target and hand/target, are the first key to accuracy.

With your hand between your eyes, the two lines overlap. If your upper arms are too heavily muscled for this between-the-eyes position to be comfortable, see how close you can get. This is the same arm position as drinking from a cup or a glass, but in this case your hand is 3 to 4 inches higher than your mouth.

2. With your eyes on your hand and the target, lower your elbow while extending your forearm gradually in a straight line to the chair. Allow your wrist to drop downward, which will rotate your fingertips toward the target. Stop the forearm extension when your thumb tip is pointing at the chair (see figure 3).

This is *accuracy*, achieved by following an imaginary line. If you didn't stay on the eye/target line but instead lowered your arm so that your fingertips covered an area of the floor between you and the chair, you would not be accurate in an actual casting presentation; your fly line would crumple and the fly would be short of the target.

Conversely, if your hand didn't stay on the line but instead traveled above it before reaching the chair, in a cast your fly line would fall back and the leader would collapse on itself. Again, the fly would be short of the target.

Now let's refine the exercise. (These instructions are keyed to right-handed folks.)

1. Start in the same position—hand between your eyes—but make a fist, with your thumb extended upward and your thumbnail at forehead level. Let's also make the target area more precise and aim for the center of the chair back.

2. Again, lower your elbow and gradually extend your forearm, but focus on your *thumb* as it travels the eye/hand/target line, ending with your hand extended so that the *tip* of your thumb overlays the chair seat.

To be deadly accurate with short casts, this stroke path, centered on the forehead, is the way to go. When we need longer strokes or other conditions negate the efficiency of this position, we move the rod hand to the right.

Figure 3: Eye/target line and hand/target line converge at the target.

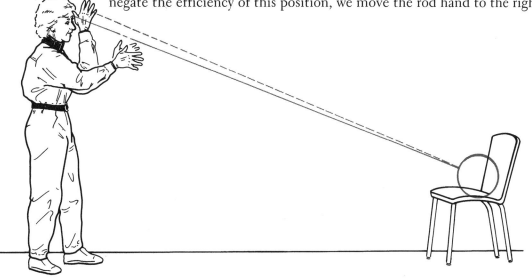

3. Retain the clenched fist at *forehead level*, but move your bent arm to the side to position your elbow in line with but ahead of your right shoulder.

Your eye/target line remains the same but your hand/target line is separate, no longer overlapping it, and so a triangle is created—an **accuracy triangle**. Hand and eyes form the base; the second and third sides are the two imaginary lines that will intersect at the target (see figure 4a).

Figure 4a: Bird's eye view of the accuracy triangle.

To make up for this separation of the two imaginary lines, think of your *elbow* as a direction indicator and line it up with the target. Now lower your elbow and extend your forearm while bending the wrist downward until your thumb tip covers the chair seat. You have moved your hand along the hand/target line and *stopped when your eyes told you to.*

The second essential element of accuracy is the positioning of the rod shaft relative to both the hand/target line and the target, before you apply the final surge of power.

Repeat the exercise but focus on your upright thumb, letting it double as the rod shaft. Move your hand along the hand/target line (2–3 inches) until your upright thumb is *perpendicular to the target area*, then thrust

Figure 4b: Rod-hand positions for power thrust to target.

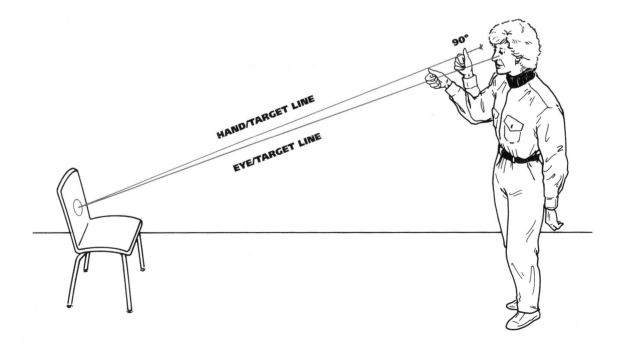

your hand forward quickly without leaving the hand/target line, meanwhile bending your wrist downward so that the tip of your thumb covers the target.

Your eyes are the master switch in fly-casting accuracy. The delightful part is that, with practice to refine your coordination, your fly rod will enable you to deliver the fly not just to a chair-seat-sized space but to a particular *inch* of the chair seat.

That's precision.

The two essential elements of accuracy are:

(1) Using the thumb/rod shaft as the indicator, move your hand along the hand/target line.

(2) When the rod shaft reaches a spot along the hand/target line that is 90 degrees from, or perpendicular to, the target, make the power thrust. The power thrust ends when the thumb tip covers the target.

CHAPTER 2

Behind the Rod

Read this chapter with a rod butt in your hand, or at least a pen or a pencil.

The Grip

The hand is the connecting link between our physical selves and our tackle. As in other sports, it must be effectively positioned to control the rod's performance.

Your grip must allow you to bring into play hand and forearm strength, and putting your *thumb on top* does this most effectively. The muscle that lies between your thumb and forefinger is then used to push the rod forward, independent of the rest of your arm, within the power application. This independent movement is an important part of casting control.

To position the thumb properly, lay the rod grip at the *base* of your fingers (not in the middle of the palm), then place your thumb on top in a *flexed* position so that its *pad*—the side opposite your nail—can be pressed against the grip (see figure 5).

The second section of your thumb must have air under it. If the thumb lies flat on the rod you must push with all of it—4 inches, perhaps. Not precise enough. To be truly effective, the pushing area should be isolated to the 1-inch thumb pad, which you use exactly as you would to push an old-fashioned round doorbell.

Not everyone can get the best out of this grip. Some have "double-jointed" thumbs, which always lie flat on the rod grip. If yours is one of these, extend your forefinger alongside the thumb and experiment to find

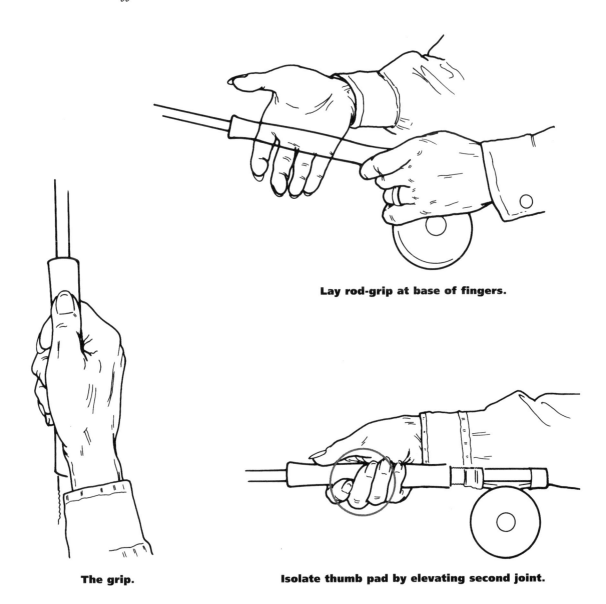

Lay rod-grip at base of fingers.

The grip.

Isolate thumb pad by elevating second joint.

Figure 5.

out which of these two positions gives you the best pushing power: thumb on top and forefinger along the side, or thumb on the side and forefinger on top.

Another factor in the correct grip position is the diameter of the rod grip. Anglers (especially women) with small hands will not be comfortable with grips that are too large in diameter; the hand will tire quickly, and abrasion and/or blisters on the heel of the hand may be an uncomfortable consequence. Have the grip sanded to reduce its diameter.

Compound Movement

Fly casting is a back-and-forth motion of the forearm and hand *within* the up-and-down motion of the whole arm.

All three parts of the casting arm come into play, and all three are used on every casting stroke: the hand moving from the wrist joint, the forearm moving from the elbow joint, and the upper arm moving from the shoulder joint. I will describe the part each plays in the casting stroke separately, but all three parts must work together to enable the casting hand to travel a *straight line* (which will be on the diagonal) on both the backcast and the forward cast.

Focus your efforts on the rod grip and the 3 or 4 inches of rod shaft just above the grip. Don't think about the midsection or tip of the rod. Each will do its job if the butt is moved along a straight line. And you can see this indicator area without taking your eyes off the target.

FOREARM ACTION

The back-and-forth motion of the forearm, in line with the upper arm, gives length to the stroke. You will use only as many inches of your maximum stroke length as are necessary, depending on the length of the line outside the rod tip. Short line, short stroke; long line, long stroke.

The angle between the forearm and upper arm will vary. Short strokes to the forehead area will create an angle of just less than 90 degrees between the two. A maximum-length stroke will bring the forearm muscle *to* the upper arm muscle but keep the hand vertical and the elbow lower than the shoulder. The forearm never moves so far back and the elbow never lifts so high as to put the hand behind the shoulder; this would throw the line downward on the backcast.

WRIST ACTION

The action of the wrist is very precise, occurring between a *bent-down* wrist and a *straight* wrist. A *bent-back* wrist would throw the fly line downward on the backcast, out of control.

A bent-down wrist is easy to describe. With your thumb on top, just push your hand downward as far as it will go, without moving your forearm. With a rod in your hand, the bent-down wrist will position the rod grip *against,* or *parallel to,* your wrist area. It's fairly common for men with well-developed wrists to have difficulty with this. If that's your case, any movement downward is acceptable; make up for the lack of flexibility by pushing forward with your thumb with added strength.

**Figure 6:
Upper-arm
motion (left):
elbow lifts
and lowers.
Forearm and
wrist motion
(right): wrist
moves between
bent-down
and straight
positions.**

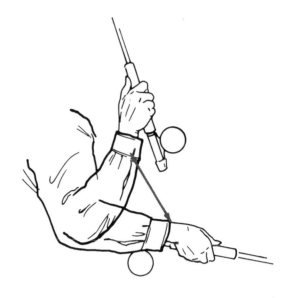

➥ Every backcast stroke *begins* with a *bent-down wrist*.

➥ Every backcast stroke *ends* with a *straight wrist*.

A straight wrist is harder to recognize unless you hold a rod in your hand. With a straight wrist, the reel-seat end of the rod grip forms a 45-degree angle with your wrist area.

➥ Every forward cast *begins* with a *straight wrist*.

➥ Every forward cast *ends* with a *bent-down wrist*.

The wrist position changes at a precise instant. More about that later.

At this point you're likely to say, "I've got it! Just pivot back and forth from the elbow, changing the wrist from bent down to straight and straight to bent down."

It is possible to pivot from your elbow and use only your forearm and hand to cast (not your upper arm) and still be very accurate, up to about 40 feet and under good conditions. But then you'll run into trouble, because this style is like running with your knees tied together. With such a restrictive arm movement, you must develop a punch to compensate. And a punch is too short and sudden an application of power to keep the line under control at all distances. Additionally, with your elbow at your side you lack leverage when casting in planes other than the vertical. Your upper arm is critical to reaching your full casting potential.

UPPER ARM ACTION

The shoulder joint lifts and lowers the upper arm; it makes the elbow move up and down. In fly casting, the maximum movement of the upper arm is between a position perpendicular to the ground—relaxed, "hanging down"—and one that's just below parallel to the ground.

How much upper arm movement do you use for a given stroke length? Let it happen naturally by moving your rod hand along the straight lines (which are diagonal) for each stroke, and letting your forearm and upper arm do what they need to do to facilitate it.

Indicators

For "indicators" of the path of the casting stroke, use your *thumbnail* on the backcast and your *thumb pad* on the forward cast.

BACKCAST: THUMBNAIL

For this exercise, you will follow a straight line from waist level to forehead level. This makes the straight line a *diagonal* and will give the proper angle to your backcast. With a bent arm and your wrist bent down, hold the rod parallel to the ground, at *waist level*. Relax your upper arm and focus on your thumbnail. Draw a diagonal line with your thumbnail to a point between your eyes at *forehead level*. At the completion, you should be looking slightly *upward* at your thumbnail.

Bringing your thumbnail up as high as your forehead automatically engages your upper arm motion. The angle of your forearm to your upper arm will be close to 90 degrees. Your upper arm will be nearly parallel to the ground. But all you had to think about was drawing a diagonal line with your thumbnail from Point A (waist level) to Point B (forehead level).

With your eye/target line and your hand/target line now overlapping for your forward cast, accuracy is easy.

FORWARD CAST: THUMB PAD

The indicator for your forward cast is your *thumb pad*. Focus on it and use it to push the rod grip along the straight line to the target until, at 90

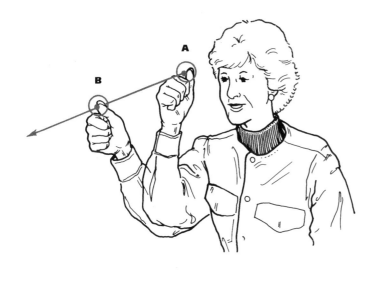

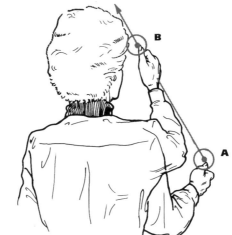

Figure 7: Thumb-pad indicator on forward cast (top); thumb-nail indicator on backcast (bottom).

degrees from the target, you thrust it forward, bending your wrist downward to end with the *tip* of your thumb pointing at the target.

Now let's move on and change the end point of your backcast. Come up from waist level but let the indicator (thumbnail) end at forehead level *in front of your shoulder*. Now the eye/target line and the hand/target line are separated, but with your hand at *forehead level* your eyes can easily determine when your thumb pad has reached the 90-degree angle on the hand/target line.

Note: I have referred to the backcast hand/target line as being on a diagonal (waist to forehead) and the forward cast hand/target line as being just "straight" between your hand and the target. But depending on your distance from the target, the forward-cast straight line may incline downward or even upward, so it, too, is diagonal.

For short fly lines the diagonal path of your thumbnail on backcasts will be to forehead level; for long lines the diagonal will be to shoulder level. On forward casts of all lengths, the diagonal will be from your thumb pad's position at the beginning of the forward cast to the target.

Note: In any forward throwing motion, it is the upper arm that positions the *elbow*, which in turn directs the forearm and hand toward the target. Your elbow must be forward of your shoulder *before* the loop that will deliver your fly is formed. Line up your elbow and you've lined up your cast.

CHAPTER 3

The Stroke

Everyone who has taken casting instruction has heard the phrase, "Let the rod do the work." How? What work?

The rod has a built-in "action"—a spring power triggered by means of the casting stroke. The stroke is the path of your rod hand in an *acceleration to a* **stop**! The spring of the rod then adds to your effort and projects the line in the form of an open-ended unrolling loop. Rod action can be described as compressed energy, waiting to go to work.

When you impulse the rod through the grip, the released power races through the decreasing diameter of the rod with increasing speed; in milliseconds the energy is transferred to the fly line and a cast is born. If you punch the rod too hard you change that smooth sequence; it's as though your muscles and the rod's muscles cancel each other out. The newborn fly-line loop is distorted and you lose control over where it will deliver the fly. An instructor's admonition to "let the rod do the work" usually means, "Slack off, don't hit it so hard!"

To engage the rod's spring action effectively, the casting stroke must **load** the rod. Loading is the bending of the rod from the tip downward and is achieved by the overall acceleration to a *stop*. Slow start, fast finish! It is the *stop* that impulses the rod to release its energy—to **unload**.

During acceleration, the butt races ahead of the tip, which lags behind under the weight of the line. When the butt is *stopped* abruptly, the tip bends downward even farther, then springs in the opposite direction (to the other side of the rod butt section), taking with it the line immediately next to the tip. This is the beginning of the new loop. The stroke is completed at the *stop* and now you wait while the new loop unrolls, using this time to *relax* before beginning your next stroke.

The speed of the acceleration and the distance over which it occurs—the stroke length—are determined by the length of the line outside the rod tip.

The Elements of the Stroke

POWER SNAP: ROD AND LINE ACTION

The heart of the casting stroke is the **power snap**. I casually introduced this to you as a "power thrust," but the term *thrust* doesn't apply to a backward motion and so I call it a power snap, good in either direction, backcast or forward cast.

The power snap is the quick movement of the rod from Point A to Point B that results in the line turning over the rod tip—from one side to the other—to form the new loop. *Snap* tells you that it's a quick movement, with a beginning and an end. *Power* describes the force or strength required to increase acceleration, over a very short distance, to an abrupt *stop!*

POWER SNAP: HAND AND ARM ACTION

The hand/wrist action on the **backcast power snap** is from a bent-down position to a straight position. At the same time the forearm is moving back

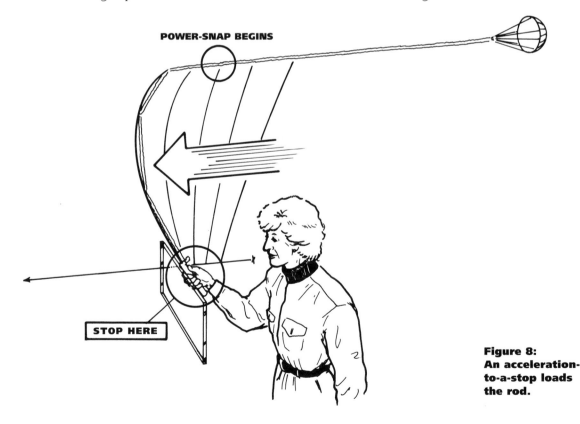

POWER-SNAP BEGINS

STOP HERE

Figure 8: An acceleration-to-a-stop loads the rod.

and the upper arm is lifting up, all taken care of by directing the power snap to forehead level with your *thumbnail indicator*.

In the forward-cast power snap, the one that delivers the fly to the target, the flexed thumb-atop-the-rod grip comes into its own. On the backcast, the hand moves as a simple unit; the wrist action is a flick or flip. On the forward power snap, the muscles of the thumb and fingers come into play to add great control to the thrust effort.

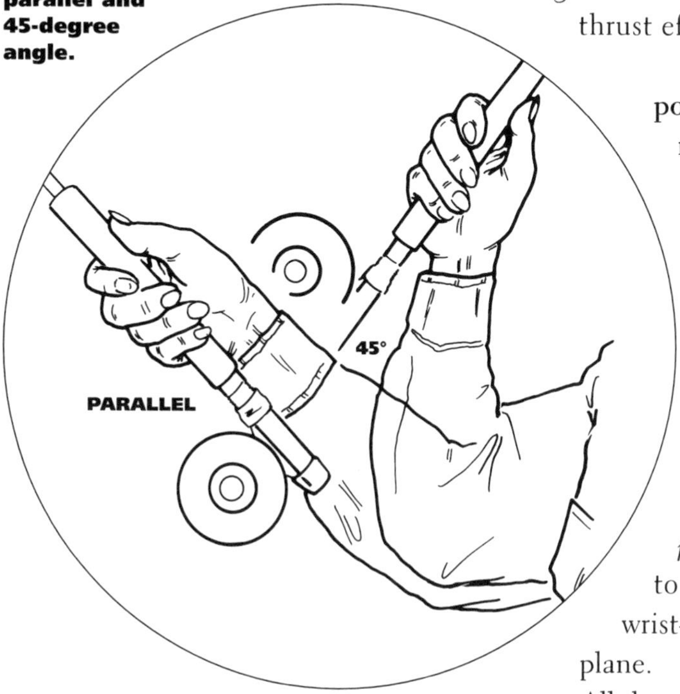

Figure 9: The Power Snap: Rod/ wrist positions between parallel and 45-degree angle.

The hand-wrist action on the **forward power snap** is similar to that used to release the latch on a screen door. With your hand in an upright position, you push a button with your thumb while applying pressure on the bar with your lower fingers (see figure 12, page 30).

From the straight-wrist position (the rod butt at a 45-degree angle to the wrist) the thumb *pushes forward sharply* while the lower fingers *pull back* on the grip to bring the rod to a position parallel to or against the wrist—a rotation of the hand in a vertical plane.

All three parts of your arm must move: Use the *thumb pad indicator* from forehead level to the target to engage them. The upper arm lowers (elbow lowers) and the forearm and hand thrust slightly but strongly toward the target.

Note: *Never* power snap to a straight arm; you may injure your elbow. Keep your arm bent and close to your body in the power snap.

LOADING MOVE

The power snap is the heart of the cast but it isn't the be-all and end-all. While it may be all you need for casts of up to 40 feet, longer casts require something additional. The power snap is brief and sudden. But if the fly line is too long for a stroke consisting only of a power snap, you'll get tailing loops.

With a **tailing loop**, instead of the loop unrolling with two parallel levels of line, the end of the fly line, along with the leader and fly, drops below the lower leg of the loop to form a "tail." One consequence is the formation of knots in your leader.

To solve the problem you must insert, ahead of the power snap at the very beginning of the casting stroke, a **loading move**. This retains the fly line's position relative to the rod tip. If the line is behind the tip (at the end of the backcast), it stays there as you begin the forward cast. If it is ahead of the tip (at the end of the forward cast), it stays there as you begin the backcast. The first move puts the rod, line, leader, and fly in motion, as a unit and under tension, and positions the rod shaft for the power snap.

The loading move only *begins* the loading of the rod; maximum loading is reached in the high-speed power snap at the end of the acceleration.

The loading move, from an accuracy standpoint, moves the rod shaft along the hand/target line to position it 90 degrees from the target, so it also doubles as a *positioning move* for the power snap.

FOLLOW-THROUGH DRIFT

To create space for a loading move *before* the power snap on the following stroke, you need a corresponding use of space *after* the power snap: the **follow-through**.

Happily, follow-through on the forward stroke is just like follow-through in other sports. After a ball is thrown or hit, your arm continues softly on the stroke path toward the target. On a forward cast, after power-snapping your thumb directly toward the target, the loop is on its way and you can relax and lower the rod in a follow-through.

Follow-through on the backcast is a different story. If you've never thrown backward, you certainly haven't followed through backward. Learning this is a challenge, but once mastered it really moves you to a higher level of proficiency. You stay connected. My late husband, Lee, called it the feeling of "constant pressure," and it is. You can feel exactly where your fly line is.

On the backcast we call follow-through by a different name: **drift**. This is a term from tournament distance fly casting that reminds you to relax while the backcast unrolls. Just as during a forward cast you follow through *forward* along the path of the stroke, on the backcast you end the power snap and then follow *back and up*, extending the imaginary line of your original stroke path.

A follow-through or drift move has no power in it. The power was applied on the power snap, determining where the fly line will unroll. *Drift time* is the time during which the fly line is unrolling; relaxing time.

HAND/WRIST ACTION DURING THE STROKE:

Backcast: Bent-down wrist on the loading move; snap to straight wrist on the power snap; retain straight wrist on the drift move.

Forward cast: Straight wrist on the loading move; snap to bent-down wrist on the power snap; retain bent-down wrist on the follow-through.

Remember that the wrist moves only on the power snap.

Figure 10:
1-2: Loading move
2-3: Power snap
3-4: Drift

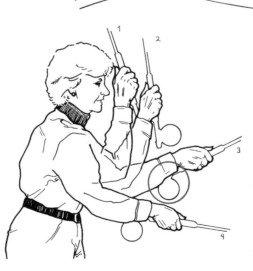

Figure 11:
1-2: Loading move
2-3: Power snap
3-4: Follow-through

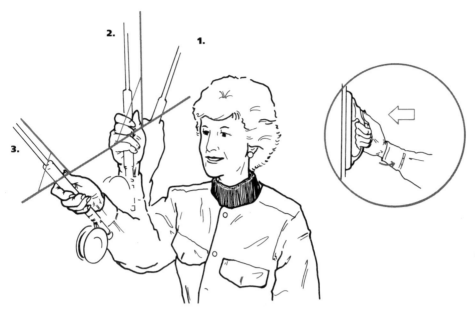

Figure 12: Power-snap positions on the hand/target line. (Inset): Screen door hand action.

Because the drift move takes you beyond the end of the power snap, your rod shaft will be farther back than 90 degrees from the target. Use the *forward loading move* to bring the rod shaft to the 90-degree position for the power snap. (The drift move backward uses the same space as the loading move forward.)

In addition to the feeling of constant pressure, this *repositioning* of the rod on the drift move enables you to start the forward stroke from a place other than where you ended the backcast stroke—invaluable both for distance casting and for eliminating false casts when changing direction. More about this later.

In summary, a casting stroke has three parts, or elements: the *loading move*, the *power snap*, and the *follow-through* or *drift*. The power snap is always the heart of the cast, executed close to your body, and, when the other two moves are used, it occurs in the center of your stroke. The space used as drift on the backcast becomes the space used for the forward-cast loading move. The space used as follow-through on the forward cast becomes the space used for the loading move on the backcast. The power snap occurs in the same place on both strokes. The three parts overlay each other.

In calm conditions, a fully executed stroke will include all three elements. If wind or obstacles become a factor, however, you may be unable to include the follow-through/drift move. This element of the stroke has no force and so has nothing to do with the acceleration to a *stop* that loads the rod and forms the loop. Because of this, I consider follow-through/drift to be outside the stroke.

Accuracy

The power snap determines exactly where the fly line will unroll and how the fly will be presented. Thus, where the power snap begins and ends on the hand/target line is all-important.

With a rod that's relatively stiff in the butt, the power snap should begin when the rod shaft, as seen just above the cork grip, is 90 degrees from—or perpendicular to—the target. It should end when the tip of your thumb is pointing directly at the target, not above or below it. Remember that the hand/target line is straight—180 degrees. Of the 90 degrees left between you and the target as you begin the power snap, you should use no more than 45 degrees for your longest casts, and less for short casts.

Rods with softer butts (which bend right down to the rod grip under the loading action) may require a few more degrees of arc—a few more inches added to the power snap—to produce the same accuracy. Begin the power snap a little earlier, perhaps 100 degrees from the target area. You'll need to experiment to see how your rod responds, but if you always think of having your thumb/rod shaft at or close to perpendicular to the target, you'll be able to refine your power-snap placement for each particular rod.

To better understand the relationship of the power snap to the angle of your fly-line loop, try this:

With 15 to 20 feet of line outside the rod tip, pretend you're standing against a clock face, with your feet at 6 o'clock and your head at 12; you're facing 9. Make a backcast that positions your fly rod's shaft to angle back beyond vertical, say to 2 o'clock. See where the line unrolls as you then power-snap forward, moving the rod shaft no more than 45 degrees *on a straight line* from the 2 o'clock position. (It will unroll 90 degrees from where you start and will have too high a trajectory to be accurate.) Power-snap from 1, 12, and 11 o'clock, and see how the angle/trajectory of the unrolling loop changes.

To be accurate at close range, which requires a low trajectory, you might begin your power snap at 11 or 12 o'clock. To be accurate at long range you will need a higher trajectory, perhaps beginning the power snap at 1 or 1:30. Beginning your power snap in a position relative to your target area is one of the foundations of accuracy.

The power snap determines where the line will go.

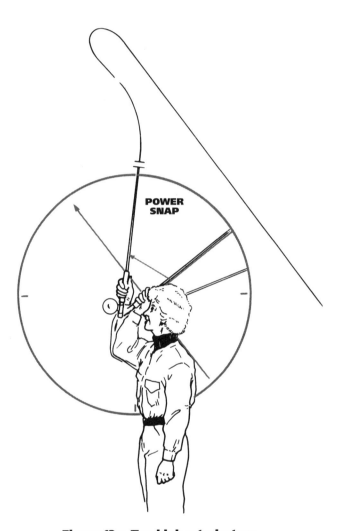

POWER SNAP

Figure 13a: Too high a trajectory.

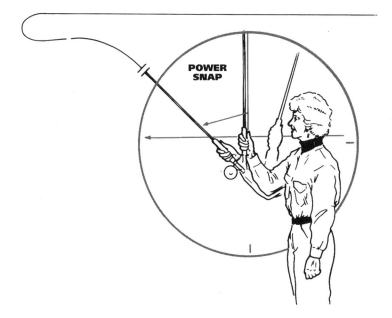

Figure 13b: For casts at medium distances.

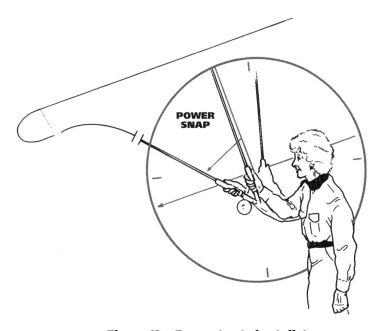

Figure 13c: For casts at short distances.

CHAPTER 4

Looking at Accuracy in Slow Motion

Fly casting is a three-dimensional sport, not easily described or understood by way of the written word.

The casting stroke I've discussed thus far is for overhead casting, and the mechanics are best learned in this vertical plane. This is the basic discipline from which you can adapt the cast to suit all possible planes and all conditions. It will be *just one* of your casting techniques.

A casting stroke also has variables that must be continuously adjusted for any change in the length of fly line outside the rod tip: *stroke length, power, line speed,* and *timing.*

And finally there is accuracy: Just as you must move your casting hand straight along the hand/target line, the fly-line loop that you form must unroll to become a straight line.

To see how all of these elements coordinate within the 180-degree parameters wherein perfect casts are made, we'll tip the whole casting action on its side, from vertical casting to horizontal casting. By casting on a grass surface you can achieve a kind of "slow motion" with each stroke and get a clear picture of just what happens in the few seconds that make or break the cast. You'll need a leader, a practice fly (use a small piece of yarn), and two objects to use as targets.

The fly line must unroll 90 degrees off the rod tip in both directions, so lay the rod on the ground, strip 20 to 25 feet of line (plus leader and fly) outside the rod tip, and carry the practice fly to the right, in line with the rod tip. Place a target about 3 feet beyond the fly.

Pick up the fly and walk it to the other side of the rod tip, straightening the fly line so that it's in line with both the rod tip and the first target.

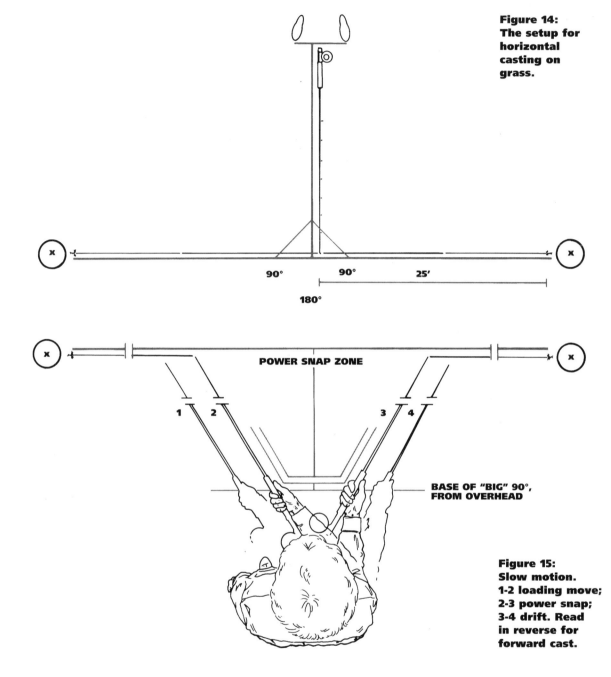

Figure 14: The setup for horizontal casting on grass.

Figure 15: Slow motion. 1-2 loading move; 2-3 power snap; 3-4 drift. Read in reverse for forward cast.

Place your second target about 3 feet farther than the length of the line, leader, and fly. These targets, in line with the rod tip, circumscribe the 180-degree parameters of the cast (see figure 14).

Stand with your feet side by side but separated, at the butt end of the rod, and pick it up. In vertical casting, you placed your thumb directly atop the grip. Retain this grip now but rotate your arm, hand, and forearm 90 degrees so that your palm is up and your thumbnail and pad are perpendicular to the ground. You will be casting horizontally, close to your body, *at waist level*. Your hand and thumb will move from side to side instead of up and down. Your forearm and upper arm will move freely to keep the path of your hand on a straight line parallel to the ground (see figure 15).

The first step is to see how the three parts of the stroke fit into this physical setup. Make just one stroke at a time and let each one land on the grass; that way you can think out what you're going to do before you do it.

The power snap is the center of your stroke. Although I have said that you begin a forward-cast power snap at 90 degrees from the target, at this point it's easier to become familiar with the stroke elements if you begin by enlarging your power snap a bit positioning its beginning and end to either side of center. "Center" means the center of your body, your belly button.

Note: Use only your rod hand when working to understand the mechanics; secure the fly line under your middle finger.

Cast any way you can to put the fly in the target area to the left.

Slow Motion

BACKCAST

For the loading move, use your thumbnail as a guide, and move your hand and rod grip (bent-down wrist) on a straight line, just a few inches, to get line, leader, and fly under tension and moving.

Power-snap to the right, ending with a strong *stop* just past center. The fly will leave the ground and the loop will form; now, as the line unrolls, follow it (let your arm *drift*) to the right. The drift move ends with the rod 45 degrees short of the target on the 180-degree line. Allow the line to land on the ground.

Of the 180 degrees you have to work with, the casting stroke uses a "big" 90 degrees. Your hand is not pivoting at the wrist to make a simple angle; the base of the arc has length (which is why I say a *big* 90 degrees), so the form is more like a U than a V.

FORWARD CAST

Before you begin, think about the length of the loading move relative to the restricted area of the power snap. Pull your elbow back toward your waist, moving the rod grip a few inches to the left (with your wrist straight), putting line, leader, and fly in motion. Power-snap on a straight line, pushing your thumb forward and pulling back on the rod grip, as with a screen door handle, from the right side of the center of your body to the left side of center. After the strong *stop*, look for the loop to form and watch it unroll,

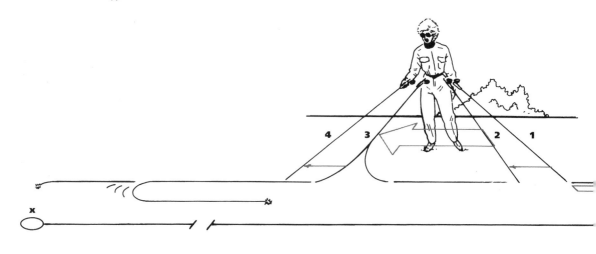

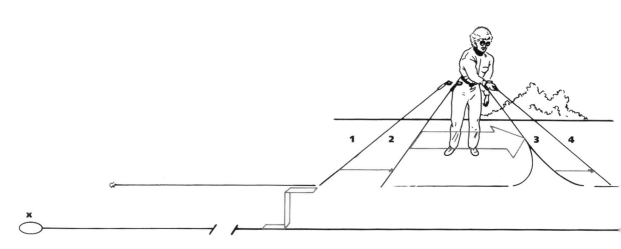

following through a few inches toward the target and, again, stopping the rod tip at no less than 45 degrees from it.

Do this over and over. This is nitty-gritty stuff and you won't be able to grasp all of the elements until you do it a few dozen times. Separate the elements of the stroke in your mind. Look for each loop to form and watch each cast unroll; learn exactly where to position the power snap to make that loop unroll the leader and fly to the target. Don't be in a hurry; this is "slow motion." You are seeing the elements that produce accuracy.

Begin each stroke with a relaxed hand, and shift your weight from side to side with the cast. Body motion simplifies the casting stroke; you don't have to move your hands as far.

**Figure 16:
Backcast at
waist level
(top); forward
cast at waist
level (bottom).**

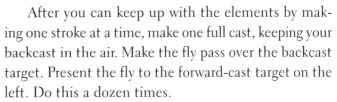

After you can keep up with the elements by making one stroke at a time, make one full cast, keeping your backcast in the air. Make the fly pass over the backcast target. Present the fly to the forward-cast target on the left. Do this a dozen times.

Now **false cast** horizontally. False casting keeps the fly line in the air; it unrolls in each direction to position the fly directly above the target, to the right and to the left. This is your accuracy check: Watch every inch of the loop's unrolling, in *both* directions.

While false casting you can see and understand the variables in the cast: *stroke length*, *power*, *line speed*, and *timing*.

Casting Variables

STROKE LENGTH

Perfect stroke length puts the fly over the target: If the stroke is too long or curved, the fly will pass behind the target; too short a stroke will send the line loop and fly forward of the target. When the stroke is the perfect length, the line loop should unroll directly to the target.

POWER AND LINE SPEED

If your fly line is not unrolling completely, your acceleration is at fault. Good line speed is seen when the line loop unrolls smoothly without falling dramatically. If there's insufficient acceleration, the line will hit the ground before it unrolls. If there is too much acceleration or too much power in the power snap, the line will contain waves and bumps and will collapse.

Perfect line speed unrolls the line, leader, and fly completely a few feet above the target. Then, with the cast's energy expended, line, leader, and fly will land lightly.

BACKCAST TIMING

How long does it take for the fly line to unroll on the backcast? The answer is, just as long as it takes for it to unroll on the forward cast, if the line length stays the same. Eventually, you'll *feel* backcast timing, subtle as it is. Casters often turn and watch their backcasts while casting in an overhead plane. However, if you turn your head more than 90 degrees to do so, you'll turn your torso and put yourself out of line; you'll be making curves with your rod hand. Casting in a horizontal plane is the way to *see* backcast timing.

Watch your backcast unroll toward the target. Begin your next stroke as the *leader* starts to unroll, because the leader and fly have no weight. The feeling of constant pressure hinges on the weight and tension of the fly line. If you wait too long, you'll feel disconnected.

Once you have everything working right—stroke length, power, line speed, and timing—*close your eyes* and turn what you saw into something you can feel!

Fly casting is a thing of feeling. The feel of this long, flexible weight is unlike anything else. It's so subtle that the best way to recognize it is to eliminate the distraction of vision. Go with the flow; trust your inner self to take over. Enjoy it! *Feeling* is the element of casting that makes it your own. Once experienced, you'll never be satisfied with anything less.

After you become familiar with this either-side-of-center power snap, reduce its size by ending your forward loading move at dead center on your body. This places your power snap's beginning at 90 degrees from the target, as you have been taught before.

Loop Control

Casting in this horizontal plane can let you play with loop size and even understand the dreaded tailing loops.

The elements of accuracy I've presented so far help you produce narrow loops—desirable for accuracy, distance, and combating winds. Narrow loops are most easily executed with weightless flies. The width of a loop is relative; even with heavy and/or air-resistant flies, you'll make the wide loops as narrow as efficiency allows.

ROD/WRIST RELATIONSHIP

Narrow loop: Keep a straight wrist until the rod shaft is positioned 90 degrees on the hand/target line, then snap to a bent-down wrist, within a 45-degree turnover arc (see figure 17).

Wide loop: Change *slowly* from a straight wrist to a bent-down wrist throughout what would have been the loading move *and* the power snap, ending with the rod shaft no more than 45 degrees from the target on the hand/target line (see figure 18).

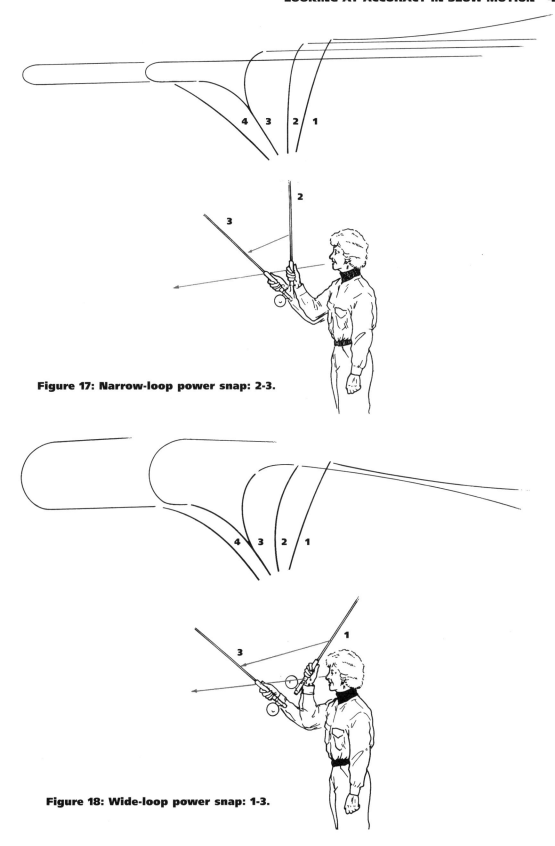

Figure 17: Narrow-loop power snap: 2-3.

Figure 18: Wide-loop power snap: 1-3.

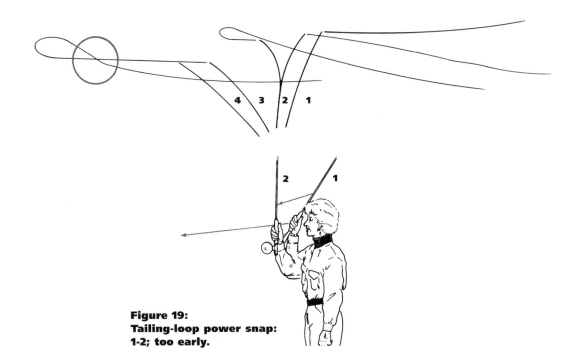

Figure 19:
Tailing-loop power snap:
1-2; too early.

As you know, the power snap creates the loop. A narrow loop is the result of no more than a 45-degree arc of the rod after the 90-degree start position on the hand/target line. Think of that 45-degree arc as the **turnover arc**.

To create a wider loop, the turnover arc must be increased to 90 degrees. The loading move is eliminated; the power snap is enlarged to encompass the whole stroke. Although the power snap will be longer, it will be *slower*. The hand/target line will remain your guide, and the lengthened power snap must still end with the rod shaft at no more than 45 degrees from the target.

TAILING LOOPS

If tailing loops are a problem, it's likely that you are leaving out the loading move and executing a short, fast power snap at the start of the stroke. Too early and too quick (see figure 19).

Horizontal casting allows you to see how this happens: Just let your backcast land on the grass, in line with the target, then power-snap it suddenly in the other direction; you'll see the end of the line, leader, and fly jump forward *under* the rod tip to form a tail or perhaps collide with the body of the line.

The few inches of movement of the loading move, before the power snap, work like magic to eliminate tailing loops and form the loop where it belongs, *over* the rod tip.

CHAPTER 5

Putting It All Together: Pickup, False Casting, Hovering, and Tension

To get the feeling of *tension* on the line that is necessary to properly begin the loading action of the backcast, you'll need to work on water.

Basic Cast: Pickup and Lay-Down

Start with your fly line completely extended. Use a roll cast (see chapter 9) on pond water; in flowing water, just point the rod downstream.

The loading move gets rod, line, leader, and fly moving as a unit toward the target area.

When you take line off the water, your backcast target area is imaginary, in the air above and behind your head. The loading move is the *lifting of the line up to the leader connection*. The power snap then *takes the leader and fly from the water*.

It is extremely important to start your stroke in the right position, one that ensures that all of the elements of your cast will fit into the space and time you have. Stand with your casting-side foot dropped back. Begin with the *rod tip lowered to just an inch or two above the water*, your elbow bent and your rod hand in a bent-down position. Relax your hand to feel the weight of the rod. Relax your body.

The loading move is a lifting of the line, *inch by inch*, but with enough speed to maintain tension on the line so that no slack forms. The bent arm, with the bent-down wrist, *lifts as a unit*, the indicator thumbnail leading the rod hand toward forehead level.

At the *instant* the line is completely off the water but the leader and fly are still on it, you can see the angle of trajectory for your backcast. This is an extension of the angle of the fly line, from the rod tip to the leader connection. The power snap then continues along this same path, projecting the unrolling backcast opposite it. This determines the "target" at which you are aiming your backcast, keeping within the 180-degree parameters.

The power-snap direction is back/up toward forehead level; the whole move occupies only as much space and time as it takes for the fly to leave the water. The wrist snaps backward from its bent-down position to a straight position.

The loading move is the longer of the two moves, because it lifts all of the fly line, which has both length and weight. It's also a "sweet" move, using *speed*, not force. The power snap is a brief *snatch!* to free the relatively short, weightless leader and fly from the tension of the water's surface.

Regardless of how much line you're picking up, it's important that your power snap ends *as* the fly leaves the water. Not a second later! Ending the power snap requires a very positive *stop!* Here, your eyes must trigger the stop.

Figure 20: Rod tip lowered (top); loading move lifts line to leader connection (middle); power snap ends as fly leaves water (bottom).

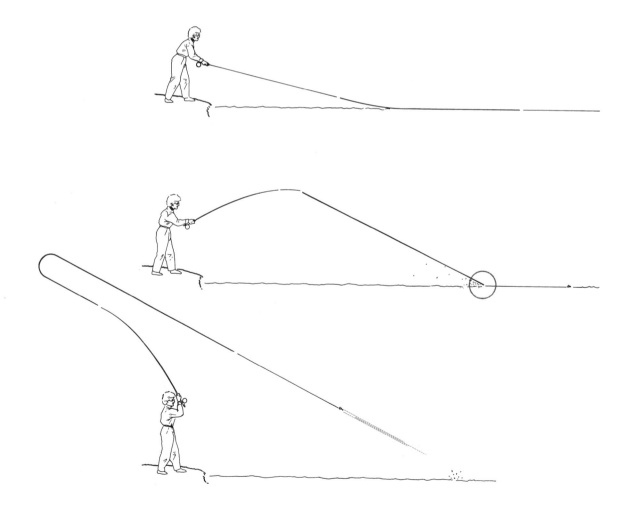

Your height and arm length, the length of the rod, and the length of the line you're picking up will determine how far your hand moves on the diagonal path from waist to forehead level. With a short line it may end a foot away from your head. As line length increases you'll need a longer stroke to lift it; therefore, the short power snap will begin and end closer to your head.

Although the stroke to get the fly off the water has two components, there can be no hesitation between them, lest line tension be lost and slack forms. The pickup is a smooth sequence, with the loading move blending into the power snap. This precise sequence produces perfect pickups for all lengths of line.

After the fly leaves the water, relax while your rod hand (in its straight-wrist position) follows through backward, extending the stroke path back and upward a few inches—the drift move. *Drift*, not force. This is also a repositioning move, creating space for your forward loading move.

The *accuracy triangle* is in place. Rock your bent arm forward (the elbow lowers) in the forward *loading move* and, when the rod shaft is 90 degrees from the target, make your power snap, to present the fly to the target inch of water.

In this basic casting discipline, the fly line should unroll completely above the water before any part of it touches down. Line, leader, and fly will land lightly, almost at the same time, depending on the length and diameter of the final tippet and the weight of the fly.

You can see from the brevity of these moves that you'll need practice to become familiar with the mechanics, the arm and hand movements, and the accuracy elements. Don't expect miracles, but take it step by step, repeating actions dozens of times until they become second nature and you can free your mind to develop overall awareness.

False Casting to Hover the Fly

You have false cast horizontally on the grass, unrolling the line from target to target. Now, when you cast overhead, your 180-degree parameter is not parallel to the water but follows a path that runs diagonally low-to-high on your backcast and diagonally to the target on your forward cast. Short casts have very high backcasts; long casts have lower ones.

When precision is all-important—when you're dropping a dry fly into the feeding lane of a rising trout, for instance, or peppering the nose of a reluctant Atlantic salmon—**hovering** a fly will let you judge exactly where it will touch on the water. Here, you increase your line speed, through a

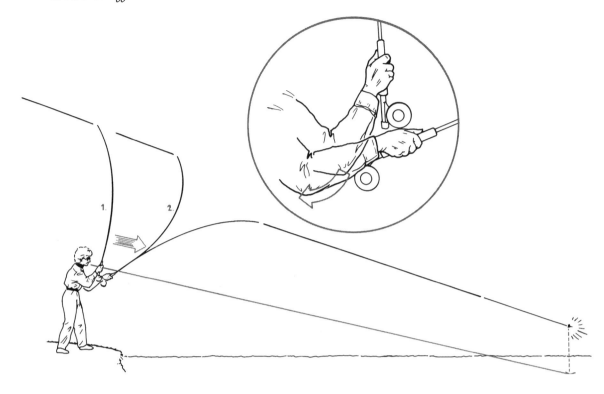

very well-defined power snap, so that the energy passes through the fly with enough speed to hold it in the air for a second.

During that second you can see exactly where the fly is relative to the target inch. If it looks right, just lower the rod or repeat the cast exactly, and drop the fly on the next one. This way you don't change your casting technique to present the fly; when you recognize the perfect false cast, that's the one you present. If the unrolling loop is at a steep-enough angle, the fly will land first.

Here again, it's the precision of your hand action, the pushing with your thumb while pulling back on the rod grip with your lower fingers, that is key to this technique. Don't stretch out the power snap; let your elbow swing back under your armpit, close to your side, and make the power snap almost in place.

Figure 21: Hovering a fly for pinpoint accuracy. (Inset): Elbow swings down and back on strong power snap.

Hand Tension

It's a bit of a shock to realize that a fly fisher makes hundreds of casts in a single day's outing. Just count the casts you make in a five-minute period. It's obvious that you'll tire very quickly if you "death-clutch" the fly rod with full muscle tension throughout every cast. This is what beginners do, and too many anglers never enter the next stage. There must be resting time in each stroke; this time occurs while the line is unrolling, during the *drift* or *follow-through*. Two resting times in each full cast! Use them.

To understand when to clutch and when to relax, hold in your hand a slightly dampened dishwashing sponge, of a size that you can compress; half of an oval-shaped sponge is ideal. Go through the casting motions with the sponge.

Backcast: On the loading move, the hand tension is firm but the sponge is not compressed. On the power snap, the sponge is compressed *fully*, then *instantly released* to expand completely during the drift move.

Forward cast: On the loading move, the sponge remains expanded but the grip starts to firm up, followed by the *full compression* on the power snap and *instant relaxation* on the follow-through.

The stroke has been described as an acceleration to a *stop!* The hand tension within the stroke can be described as increasing in firmness to a final instant of full compression. The follow-through/drift is *outside* the stroke, and is therefore relaxing time.

Figure 22: On both strokes full tension is reached only at the end of the power snap (3), followed by immediate relaxation (3a).

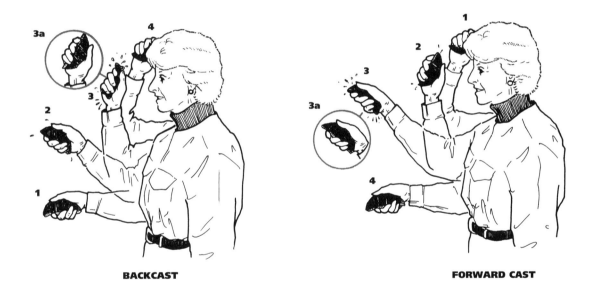

BACKCAST   FORWARD CAST

Shoulder Tension

Tension in the shoulder of the casting arm can make you unable to perform the casting mechanics I have described. Shoulder tension keeps the rod hand from being brought back close enough to the head area. Consequently, the upper arm is lifted then kept stationary, so that the forearm and hand pivot on the elbow much too high in the air.

The shoulder must be relaxed enough to bring the hand back close to the forehead or shoulder. The best analogy I can come up with is the act of drinking, mentioned earlier. You lift a cup or glass and bring it to your lips, without tension in your shoulders. I ask you to bring your thumbnail to your forehead, which is above your lips but on the same face!

This problem of shoulder tension is much more common among men than women, in my teaching experience. Men are naturally more heavily muscled in the upper body than are women. They're accustomed to using their strength in sports activities and take longer to recognize that casting a fly rod requires more finesse than pure strength. I often suggest that a male student use only one-quarter of the strength he is using to cast badly in order to cast well. It works.

Figure 23: Relaxed shoulder allows the rod hand to come close for better control.

Shoulder tension hampers the backcast.

CHAPTER 6

Accuracy in All Planes, Forehand and Backhand

It's time to look at the real world of fly casting under fishing conditions. In any fishing experience, obstacles in the form of trees and bushes, wind, and even being on the wrong side of the river force us to switch constantly between forehand and backhand casting.

Basically, we must be able to cast accurately at all angles between horizontal on the right and horizontal on the left. Look directly at a clock face for reference: 12 o'clock is vertical and, for a right-hander, everything between 12 and 3 can be considered **forehand** casting; between 12 and 9 it can be called **backhand** casting.

Positioning of the feet can be important: casting-side foot *back* for forehand casts, casting-side foot *forward* for backhand casts.

I've already covered casting vertically (12 o'clock) and horizontally (3 o'clock). Your thumb is upright at the 12 o'clock position, and your palm is up at 3. You can accommodate any forehand angle between these—casting at 1 o'clock, 2 o'clock, or in between—by tilting your forearm and hand outward, with elbow in, to make casts. Whatever the angle, make straight lines back and forth from where you begin, and maintain the 90-degree positioning of the beginning of the power snap for accuracy.

Backhand casting appears difficult and, perhaps by relating it to a tennis backhand, many anglers overcompensate by reaching across their bodies, positioning the rod hand as far left as possible. Because of the rod's length, however, you don't need to take your rod hand to the left of your body. The secret to backhand casting easily and accurately is to *swing the elbow outward* to tilt the *rod tip* to the left of center, but to *keep the rod hand as close to the center of your head as possible.*

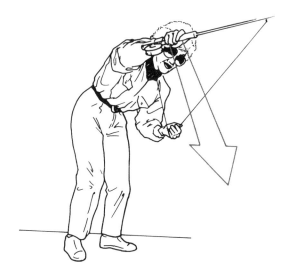

Figure 24a: Taking the hand to the left of your face reduces control.

Figure 24b: This is a good position for backhand control.

To cast at 11 o'clock, swing your elbow outward to position your forearm, thumb, and rod at that angle. Keep your hand at forehead level and *just a few inches from your face.* Once more, your eye/target line and your hand/target line are overlapping, and accuracy is easy.

To cast in a plane lower than 11 o'clock, you'll be accurate if you keep your thumb at forehead level and bend sideways, from the waist, to maintain the overlapping eye/hand/target line; the lower the angle, the higher your elbow. At 9 o'clock your forearm will be parallel to the water; your palm will face downward.

By keeping your rod hand at forehead level for these low-angle targets, you can *see* it moving back and forth over the necessarily short, straight line between you and the

Figure 25: Rotation of the elbow positions the rod hand for all planes.

target. Use the thumbnail and thumb pad for your indicators. If your hand makes a straight line, in line with the target area (under overhanging branches, for instance), the rod tip will travel that line and the loop will unroll in the same plane to deliver the fly to the target.

The hand's path is one key; beginning the power snap 90 degrees from the target is the other.

By being able to cast in this full spectrum, from horizontal on the right to nearly horizontal on the left, you can choose to execute a cast with both strokes in the same plane, or with a change of planes between backcast and forward cast. This is helpful both at the end of a fished-out cast, when you need to change direction to present the fly again, or to cope with wind.

Changing Planes within the Cast: Use of Drift Time

To change planes between backcast and forward cast, you must know exactly where your power snap ends so that you can reposition your rod hand *while the line is unrolling*. I define this as **drift time**, because time is the restriction.

As an example, if the wind is blowing from your casting side, you can make the backcast on that side, but the line will be blown into you on the forward cast. To solve this problem, again think of a clock face. You could make the backcast with the rod angled at 1 or 2 o'clock (depending on where you have to start from), and the forward cast at 11 o'clock.

As soon as you have ended the power snap with its positive *stop* at 1 or 2 o'clock, *reposition* your rod hand to 11 o'clock for the upcoming forward cast. Just move your hand left to forehead level close to your face, rotating your elbow outward/upward a bit, as described earlier (see figure 26).

If you false cast—perhaps to facilitate a backhand presentation—use the forward **follow-through time** to reposition for the coming backcast. In the above example, having made the forward power snap at 11, you'll need to rotate your forearm and hand to the right, after the power snap, to make another backcast at 1 o'clock. You'll be switching between forehand and backhand casting on each full cast. With the repositioning moves, the whole action becomes elliptical.

Practice this changing of planes by using the clock face as a reference; choose two numbers between 9 and 3 (one for the backcast and one for the forward cast) to combine into a full cast. The smaller angles of change are of course easier, but if you make a mental diagram of what you hope to do and position your body for the freedom to do it, you'll be surprised at

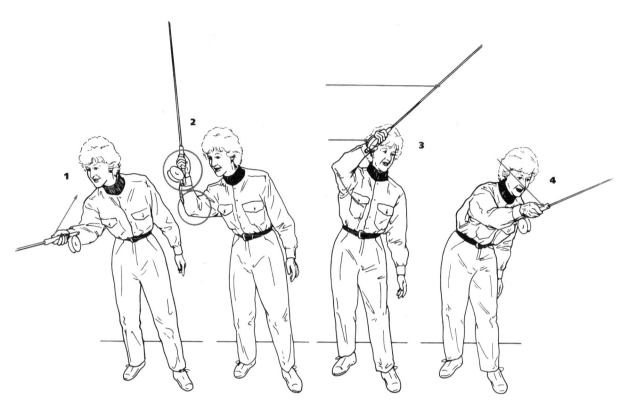

what you can accomplish with the drift repositioning move, even in tough wind conditions. Remember that all your maneuvering must be completed before your presentation power snap begins. That move must be a straight line to the target.

The ability to cast in different planes, and the use of drift and follow-through time to reposition between the separate strokes, will give you great confidence in your ability to be accurate under all conditions.

Figure 26: For change of direction, reposition the rod between back and forward power snaps (2-3: drift time).

CHAPTER 7

Shooting Line and Double Hauling

Fly casting does, of course, include the use of your second hand. I have purposely ignored it until now because improper use of the line hand can slow the learning process.

The **rod hand's** responsibilities are the casting mechanics: loading move, power snap, and follow-through; and the variables: stroke length, power, line speed, and timing. These should be so familiar as to be second nature before the line hand is added.

The **line hand's** responsibilities are keeping slack from forming between this hand and the rod's first guide; stripping line from the reel; holding line; releasing line or stopping its release on the shoot; retrieving line; and hauling (as in single or double hauls).

An additional chore for the line hand is keeping the fly line from fouling on the rod handle, the reel, or your vest. It is in your best interest to become aware of your line hand's location at all times. Start by keeping your hands separated by 10 to 12 inches.

Shooting Line

Shooting line accomplishes the magic of a presentation cast longer than the line held in the air. This enables us to reach targets that are otherwise out of our range, and with a minimum amount of effort.

Begin training the line hand by moving it in coordination with the rod hand, but at a slightly lower level. When the rod hand moves upward toward the forehead the line hand should move correspondingly upward, but at its peak it will be a few inches lower.

Figure 27: Line hand tension: moving your hands in unison is key.

On the forward cast, the line hand maintains tension on the fly line so that no slack forms while the hands move in unison, parallel to each other.

Extending a cast by shooting line requires a change in speed and power. The backcast preceding the shoot should receive an extra bit of *power* and the fly line, leader, and fly be allowed to unroll *completely*. This will produce a tiny *tug* on the line. This tug "preloads" the rod—its tip is already bending back as the forward cast begins. The forward stroke, too, requires *more power* and has to be made at a slightly higher angle (just an inch or two), to allow the longer line room to unroll above the water.

The time to release line for shooting is *after* the power snap has been completed and the line loop formed. Early release will open up the loop, dissipating the energy. A visual aid is to look upward and see line ahead of the rod tip before releasing.

The accuracy rules still apply when shooting line. The power snap must be positioned to start at 90 degrees from the target. As the fly line unrolls, you must see the potential extension of the loop in relation to the target area. Your line hand is now in control in presenting the fly with accuracy; stop the flow of line when your eyes tell you.

Line can also be shot on the backcast, after the power snap. This is done easily with weight-forward lines and when the weighted section of your weight-forward line is just outside the rod tip. For your longer casts it is most effective to shoot several feet of line backward, but *only* on the final back-cast, the one before presentation.

Hauls

A **haul** is the action of the line hand opposite the rod hand's power snap. It is made in precisely the same time and same length as the power snap, but its direction is *opposite* that of the power snap. Hence, if your back-cast power snap is a back/up motion, your line hand's haul should be for-ward/down. On the forward power snap, made directly toward the tar-get area, the haul should be a back-ward movement ending next to your left thigh. These precise locations keep the line clear of all obstacles in the rod-grip area.

Done correctly, hauls create one beautiful instant of tension in the rod, at the peak of the loading action. Hauls maximize the loading action; the deeper the load on the rod, the more energy created by the spring power. Higher levels of energy create higher line speed, in the unrolling

Figure 28: Hauls maximize the loading action, creating one beautiful instant of tension.

loop, which is valuable in casting against wind or going for distance.

Casting in the horizontal plane, on grass, is the ideal way to learn the double haul, because it allows you to isolate the technique's components.

DOUBLE HAULS

In the first stage of learning a **double haul**, move both hands parallel to each other on the *loading move*, haul line in through the rod (shorten what

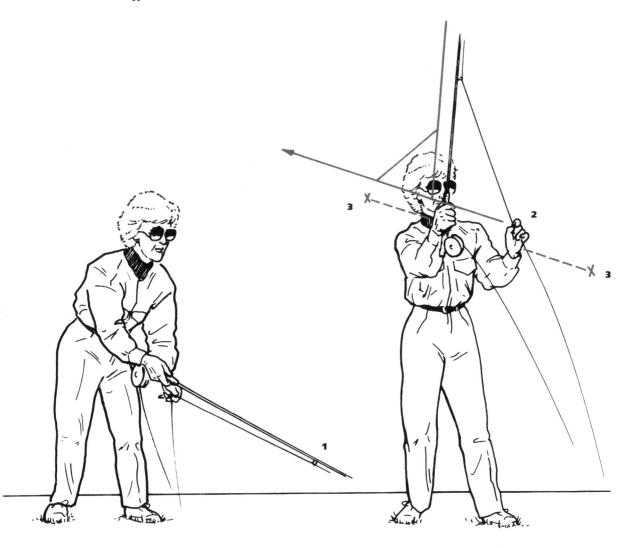

Figure 29a: Beginning position

Figure 29b: End of loading move

Figure 29c: Poor hauling form: line can catch on clothing or reel.

Figure 29d: End of power snap—note the line-hand elevation.

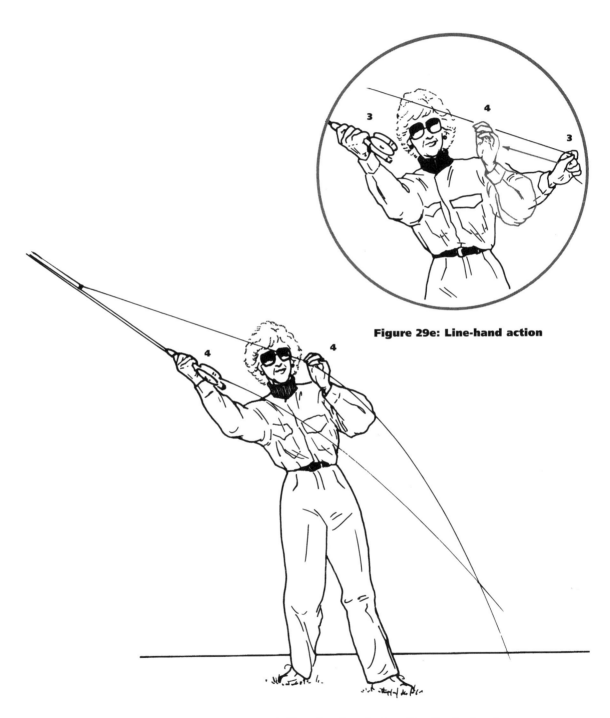

Figure 29e: Line-hand action

Figure 29f: Rod hand drifts; line hand gives line back slowly.

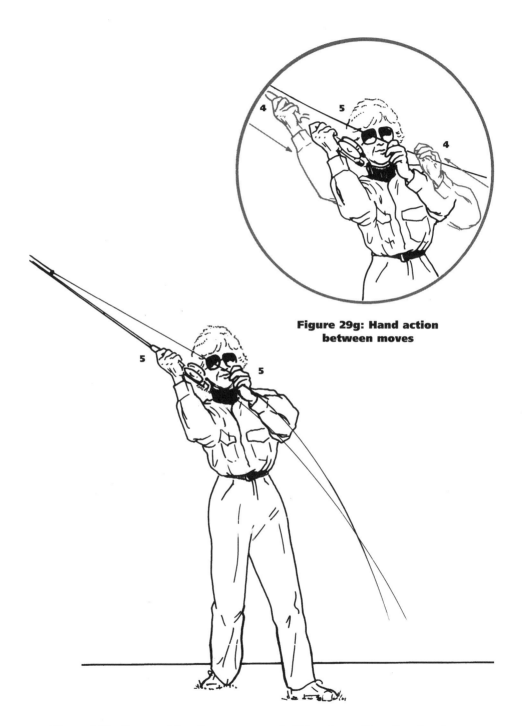

Figure 29g: Hand action between moves

Figure 29h: Forward loading move: rod slides down line; line hand continues to move up.

Figure 29i: Line is released.

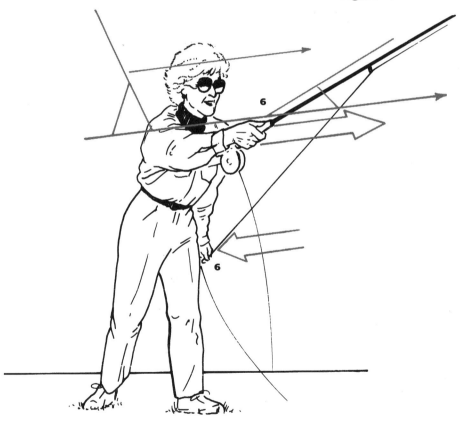

Figure 29j: Power snap and haul.

is outside the rod tip) on the backcast *power snap*, then allow that line to slide back out through the rod during *drift time*. Pull in, give back. On the forward stroke you repeat this action, pulling in line on the power snap and giving back line during the follow-through time.

After isolating the haul/power snap coordination in slow motion on the grass, move up to false casting while hauling. For this you'll need a new awareness, a second stage of performance: You will "give line back," *not* all at once while the loop unrolls, but *only at the speed that keeps tension on the line*, in the area between your hand and the first guide. You don't give back line entirely on the drift move but instead give it back much more slowly through *both* the drift move *and* the forward loading move. At one point in the execution your two hands will be moving toward each other, the rod sliding down the fly line. I call this **slide loading**.

This timing is controlled by *feeling*, and your two hands have entirely separate jobs in the few seconds between the backcast power snap and the forward-cast power snap. The line hand never travels above the reel but reaches a position just below it in time for the forward power snap.

Again, your rod hand's movements must be second nature before you work on double hauling so that your mind is free to concentrate on the line hand.

SINGLE HAULS

A single haul is not half a double haul. It's a technique used primarily when the wind is at your back and you can't use a double haul.

In a **single haul**, you again coordinate the haul with the power snap: Move line through the rod (pull it *in*) but *do not give it back*. You haul, then maintain tension while the line unrolls. A single haul may be used on the backcast only, on the forward cast only, or on both strokes. Single hauling on both strokes is a perfect technique for fishing with heavy flies in a back wind. You don't "give the line back" (the wind won't let you) but instead make the first haul on your backcast and hold the position; then, on your forward cast, make a second single haul, starting where the first one ended, followed by a release of the line.

Hauls make the rod hand's job easier, reducing by about half the stroke length needed to cast a given amount of line. This, plus the added line speed generated, makes hauling a technique valuable under various conditions with short or long lines.

Longest Casts

You will probably use double hauls for your longest casts, and here another area of awareness needs to be explored. For your longest casts, the angles of the strokes' path are as follows: The backcast should be aimed to start unrolling about 30 degrees *above horizontal* (around 2 o'clock). As the long line unrolls, it should fall to *just below horizontal* (3:30–4 o'clock). High line speed is required to keep it from falling too low.

This backcast path will be *opposite* the upcoming forward-cast angle, which should be high, 30 degrees or so above horizontal (10 o'clock on the clock face). Your forward power snap will once again begin 90 degrees from the target area on this upwardly angled hand/target line. And the elbow will *lift* on the power snap.

The form of this long-line cast is an **X** on its side (see figure 30).

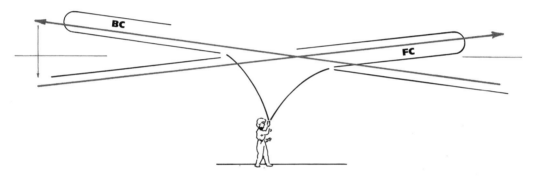

Figure 30: Long cast trajectories. BC = Backcast path; FC = Forward cast path.

CHAPTER 8

Lining Up

Your stance affects your ability to cast accurately. Proper alignment of the body relative to the target controls direction and facilitates full arm movement. Your rod hand must be able to travel the straight path of the hand/target line without restriction.

With two basic stances—one for vertical casting and one for off-vertical casting—you can confidently handle all conditions. Vertical casting is better for push-button accuracy because of its close eye/hand/target alignment. Off-vertical casting is much more versatile, however. Use it for your longest casts while deep wading, casting heavy or air-resistant flies, or fishing under troublesome wind conditions. You'll need to be skilled in both stances, switching between them as conditions dictate.

Stance 1: Square to the Target

In overhead casting, the torso faces the target throughout the cast. The casting plane is "vertical." The backcast power snap ends with the rod hand's thumb between the center of the head and the outside edge of the casting shoulder (see figure 31). The drift move is back/up. This is the same plane used when chopping wood—up and down.

For short casts, stance is unimportant. Either foot can be forward or the two can be side by side (see figure 32). As your line length increases, however, along with your stroke length, you need body motion, and now stance becomes important. Body motion is simply the shifting of weight from front foot to back foot on the backcast and from back to front on the forward cast. The foot corresponding to your casting hand should be dropped back behind the other and turned outward by 45 degrees (see figure 33).

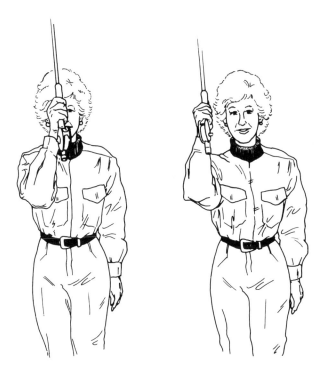

Figure 31: Stance: square-to-the-target for vertical plane casting.

For your longest strokes in this vertical casting stance, bend forward at the waist, leaning over the rod, before you begin the pickup. Shift your weight during the stroke; the completed weight shift coincides with the end of the power snap. Keep your weight back while the line unrolls during the drift move, then start the forward-cast weight shift with your forward loading move.

Stance 2: Sideways to the Target

In off-vertical casting, with the rod tilted outward at a 45-degree angle, you need a different stance, one that allows you to rotate your torso between "square" and "sideways" to the target.

The foot on the casting side is dropped back but *turned outward* 90 degrees from the other. The rod is angled at 45 degrees, or 1:30 on a clock face. The hand, too, is 45 degrees off vertical, the palm halfway between palm sideways and palm up. Do this by tilting your forearm and hand outward, keeping your elbow in close and *forward* of your shoulder.

For short casts in this off-vertical plane, the torso can remain square, or almost square, to the target, as explained in chapter 6.

For long casts, torso rotation comes into play. To take a long line off the water in this stance, start with your upper body facing the target and

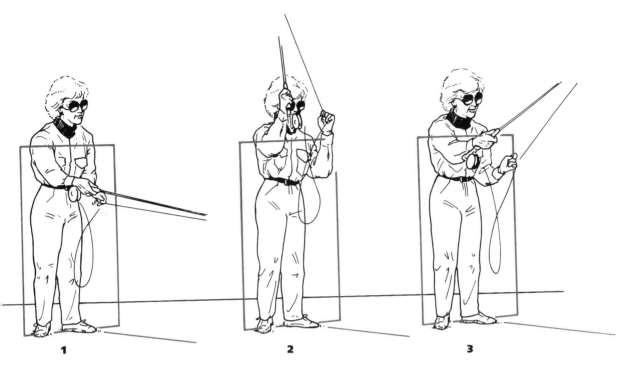

Figure 32: Square-to-the-target for short casts requires up and down motion and no weight shift.

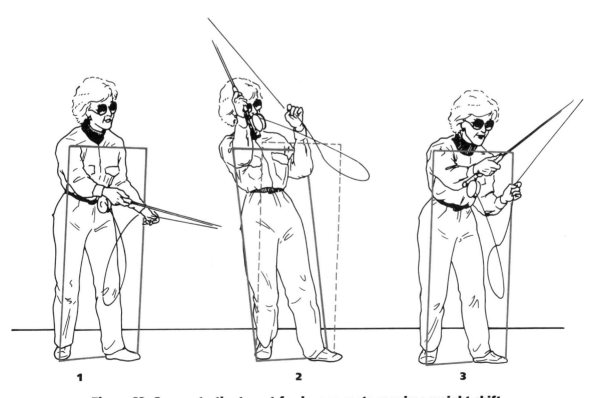

Figure 33: Square-to-the-target for longer casts requires weight shift.

Figure 34: Sideways-to-the-target for off-vertical casting plane requires torso rotation and weight shift.

thumbnail facing upward. As you lift the rod and line on the loading move, start to *rotate* your torso to move your casting shoulder rearward while also *rotating* your arm and hand to the 45-degree off-vertical position in preparation for the power snap.

The power snap is again a diagonal movement. Your rod hand should end in a position no farther back than even with your shoulder. The elbow remains forward; don't swing it outward!

The end of the rotation and the weight shift coordinate exactly with the end of the power snap. Drift in this stance moves your elbow away from your body in a straight line (to the right rear for a right-hander), and your extended but bent forearm will be *in line* with your shoulders. At this point you can turn your head and *see* your forearm, hand, rod, line, leader, fly, and the unrolling fly line *all lined up*. No harm results from looking at your backcast in this stance; it can actually help. The fly line should be unrolling 90 degrees off the tip of the angled rod. If it's behind you, you've swung out your elbow or raised your forearm vertically.

On the forward-cast loading move, your elbow leads your forearm back into the body, moving your rod hand to its 90 degrees-from-the-target position. Make the power snap within the 45-degree parameters on the hand/target line. Shift your weight and rotate your torso once again so that your shoulders are square to the target just at the end of the power snap.

To false cast in this position, the torso rotation shifts your shoulders back and forth between the two positions: square to the target, then sideways to the target, then square to the target. This is easier to do than it reads; it makes physical sense.

Body Blocks

Not all of us possess sheer strength. According to military-services information released as long ago as the mid-1980s, women have roughly 55 percent of the strength of men, pound for pound. Although this figure may not be completely accurate, it does help to explain why there are so few women of my generation (born 1926) in the world of fly fishing. The tackle of those days was too heavy, both bamboo and the later fiberglass. Now most rods are made of graphite, and although lighter rods are available to do any job, women must take on the responsibility of finding them. Men, understandably, may recommend rods that are too heavy.

All of this means that we must use whatever strength we have very precisely. **Body blocks** are the best technique to use in doing this. Men should take advantage of these techniques as well. Many anglers begin having shoulder problems as they near age sixty; this could be a consequence of using overly heavy tackle and/or casting in a way that unduly stresses the shoulder.

When making long casts, especially with heavier rods and lines, we need long strokes, great speed, and strength. Our greatest strength is when moving forward; we have available all of the hand muscles on the forward power snap. On the backcast power snap our wrist "flicks" from bent down to straight, with only the squeezing of the hand and forearm muscles to end it. Thus the need for body blocks is on the *backcast power snap.*

I use two body blocks: a weight shift using the strength of the legs, and blocking the forearm muscle against the upper arm muscle.

STANCE 1: SQUARE TO THE TARGET, VERTICAL CASTING

Position your feet as shown in figure 35a. On your backcast, your weight shift must end *precisely* with the end of your power snap, pressuring your back foot to "grab" the surface on which it stands and exerting a downward pressure on your bent knee to stop any further movement.

In this vertical casting plane, the forearm comes back in line with, and to, the upper arm; *the two muscles touch.* The elbow swings forward/up slightly with the force of the stop, and the thumb remains upright.

**Figure 35a:
Body blocks
square-to-the-
target (vertical
plane).**

**Figure 35b:
Body blocks
sideways-to-
the-target (off-
vertical plane).**

STANCE 2: SIDEWAYS TO THE TARGET, OFF-VERTICAL CASTING

Position the feet as shown in figure 35b. Again, the weight shift and bent-knee pressure reinforce the end of the power snap.

The diagonal path of your thumb in this plane (1:30 on the clock) ends even with—but just outside—your shoulder. As your forearm moves backward you must keep your upper arm and elbow *forward* and very close to the body. The upper arm's forward position *blocks* the forearm's backward movement and stops it strongly, absolutely, and without any strain.

These blocks are the stand-alone techniques that first enabled me to cast long lines with heavy tackle. They are a discipline that I cannot do without, one that will enable me to make my longest casts for the rest of my fly-fishing life.

CHAPTER 9

The Roll Cast

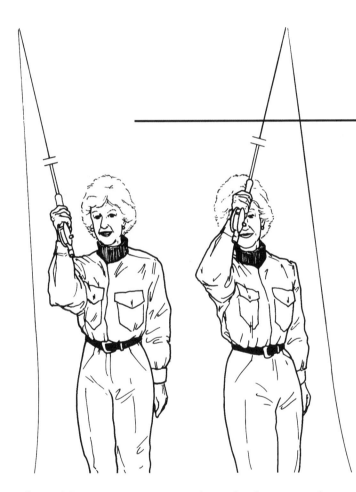

In fishing situations that preclude an aerial backcast, the roll cast comes to the rescue. With only a foot of space between you and the trees, bushes, or other obstacles, you can transform a pile of slack line into a straight cast. And it's easy: You use one stroke instead of two, and that one is a forward stroke.

Before you can roll cast forward, you must set up in a position emulating the end of a backcast. Raise the rod slowly upward, moving your thumbnail on its path toward your forehead. As you do so, focus on the line hanging between the rod tip and the water.

Figure 36: Roll-cast Setup: Forehand: elbow in (left). Backhand: elbow out (right).

You must draw this line toward you to a position that bellies it behind the rod and your shoulder.

Tilt arm, hand, and rod to the 1:30 off-vertical position, to keep the line from colliding with the rod. Your thumbnail should be at forehead level, just to the right of your head; your wrist should be straight (a 45-degree angle with the rod butt). Let the moving line come to a complete stop and put your weight on your back foot.

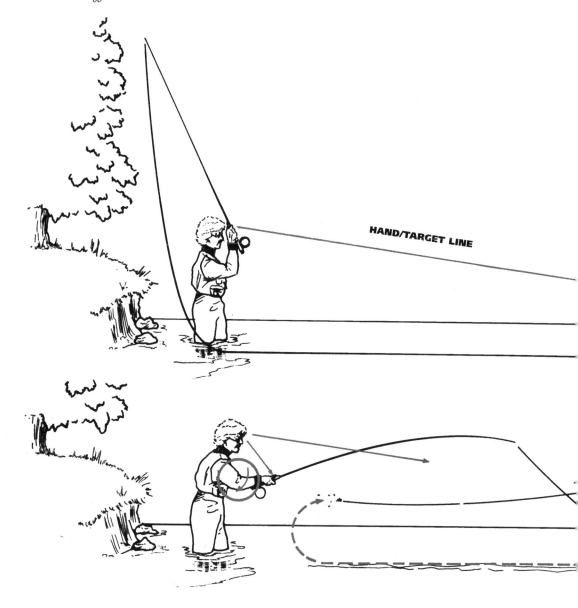

Take all the time you need to set up in this position.

To be *accurate*, line up your elbow with the particular inch of water on which you wish to present your fly. Keep your arm bent as you start the thumb pad on its hand/target path, lowering your elbow. When the shaft is perpendicular to the target inch, power-snap forward.

You may vary the elevation of the line's unrolling. To unroll *on* the water, drop *below* the hand/target line on the stroke. This is a "chopping" move, like chopping wood with an ax or pounding meat with a tenderizing tool.

Figure 37: The stroke is made BELOW the hand/target line to unroll the line ON the water.

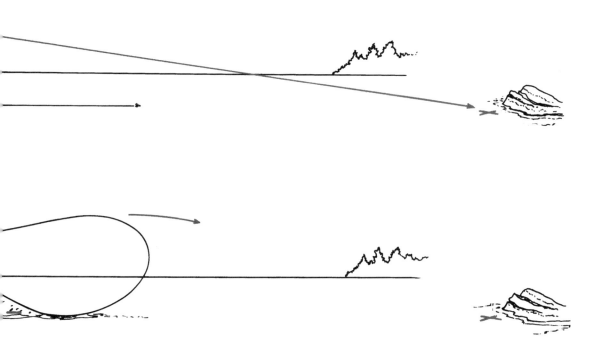

The elbow lowers and moves back under the shoulder. If you wish to unroll the line above the water, perhaps to present a dry fly, stay *on* the hand/target line. With a long tippet that you wish to pile up, aim *above* the hand/target line. It's yours to determine.

Shooting line with a roll cast is a bit tougher than with an aerial backcast. It requires practice. Tip the scales in your favor by trying it first with a strong back wind. Travel the hand-target line for the trajectory you want (above horizontal) and add a single haul, coordinated exactly with the power snap.

Roll Pickup

If there's slack in your line when you're ready to pick it up from the water, the **roll pickup** is another valuable technique. Set up as you would for a standard roll cast, but make the target a spot in the air 6 feet above the water, and roll to it. This becomes in effect a false cast; follow it with a standard backcast and go on into your presentation.

CHAPTER 10

Accuracy under Fishing Conditions

You may think that being precise will make you rigid, unbending, always following rules. But rules are a base, a guide; the idiosyncrasies of your tackle, your body, and even your personality will influence how rigidly you follow them. If it works, it's yours; cast with confidence.

We fish water and we fish fish. For trout, salmon, and steelhead we fish the water. The challenge is to put the fly in both general and precise areas. How do the elements of accuracy get bent when we want to puddle a cast or have the leader fall back on itself? How do we repeat a cast exactly?

For largemouth and smallmouth bass we fish the water, presenting the fly close to an obstacle of some kind: shoreline clutter, submerged logs—*structure*. Do we want the fly line to unroll above the water or on the water?

Bonefish, tarpon, permit, and other species found on saltwater flats must be hunted before the fishing begins. Here we fish fish! As moving targets they have to be led, as in trap-, skeet, and wing shooting. How can we be accurate?

Let's apply the accuracy elements to fishing patterns.

Trout, Salmon, Steelhead

DOWNSTREAM WITH STREAMERS, WET FLIES, OR WAKING (SKIDDING ON THE SURFACE) FLIES

Accuracy is general in these situations; you are covering water. The cast should extend fully to the far side of the current and "swim" across it. A fish that strikes at but misses the fly presents an accuracy challenge, however, but one that's easily met because, having chosen the spot in which it was lying to feed, the fish can be expected to return to it.

You need to reproduce the cast—easily done if you have marked your lines with a waterproof marker. Put a 1-inch mark on the line at 30 feet, two 1-inch marks at 40 feet, and three at 50 feet. With these references you can cover any fish's lie again, and perhaps adjust the speed of the fly with a *mend* (lift and roll the bulk of the line back against the current). With marked lines, you can even rest a fish or leave the spot, then come back later to try again.

UPSTREAM WITH DRY FLIES

This is accuracy territory. Whether they're rising or not, you know where the fish should be lying. Your targets become seam edges (where fast and slow currents parallel each other), pockets ahead of and behind rocks, the edges of eddies, the food lanes defined by bubbles or foam, undercut banks, and so on.

Accuracy principles come into their own with rising fish. Know the characteristics of your leader. With a short tippet the cast will extend the leader fully, making it easy to hover the fly for pinpoint accuracy.

With a long tippet, designed to collapse on itself for a longer drag-free float, you'll want to research the way it uncoils relative to a taking point, until you know exactly where your target area must be.

To repeat a dry-fly cast exactly, marked lines will help. Reel in all of the unnecessary fly line, during the cast, make sure both hands move in unison so the line is neither shortened nor lengthened and the presentation stroke ends at exactly the right height.

To *puddle* a cast, where the leader collapses on itself, you must aim the leading edge of the unrolling loop to hit the water before it fully unrolls. "Mechanically," your thumb pad indicator follows a path below the hand/target line, and you lessen the acceleration. Finding how steep the diagonal of the power snap should be and how much you should decrease your acceleration may require a little experimentation until you develop a sixth sense. Experimentation is broadening; it teaches you subtleties.

A second technique for puddling is to aim the cast well above the hand/target line, then lower the rod tip quickly, making the end of the line, the full leader, and the fly fall back on themselves. This is a good downstream technique for dry flies.

The *reach cast* is inherently valuable for delaying drag with dry flies. After the power snap, during follow-through, swing the rod upstream (*reach*

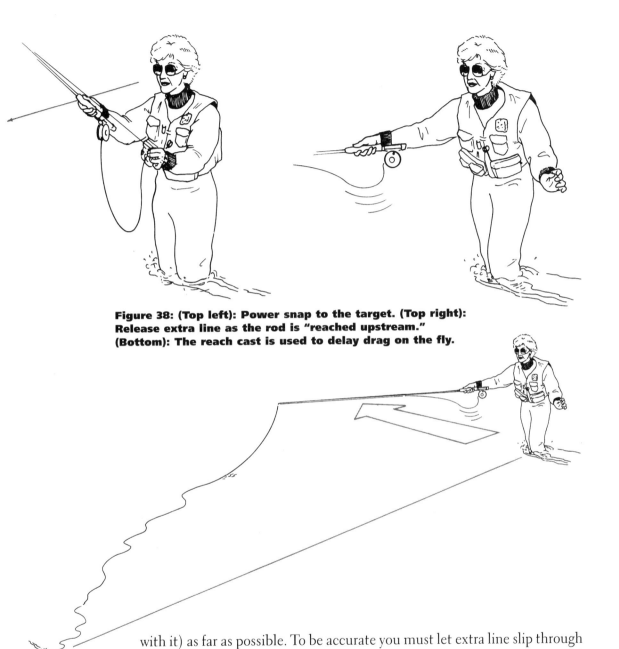

Figure 38: (Top left): Power snap to the target. (Top right): Release extra line as the rod is "reached upstream." (Bottom): The reach cast is used to delay drag on the fly.

with it) as far as possible. To be accurate you must let extra line slip through the rod while making the reach move; otherwise you will end up short of the target area (see figure 38).

UNDER OVERHANGING BRANCHES

Successfully presenting a fly in tight places, such as under overhanging branches, means learning to cast in all planes. Choose the low angle needed, power-snap at the 90-degree mark, and don't chicken out and

**Figure 39:
Overhanging
branches
require a
low-angle cast.**

waver off the hand/target line just because the loop is unrolling under a
tree limb. The tighter the target area, the less room there is for deviation
from the discipline.

WITH WEIGHTED NYMPHS

Use the loading move to lift the line and leader right up to the weighted
fly for the pickup; make a slow, soft power snap to take the fly from the
water. Let the line, leader, and fly fully unroll. On the forward cast, enlarge
the power snap by beginning it ahead of the 90-degree mark on the hand/tar-
get line—again, softly and slowly.

Bass

Surface bass flies are presented next to obstacles, in shoreline indentations,
between lily pads, and so on. The air-resistant surface flies should be lifted

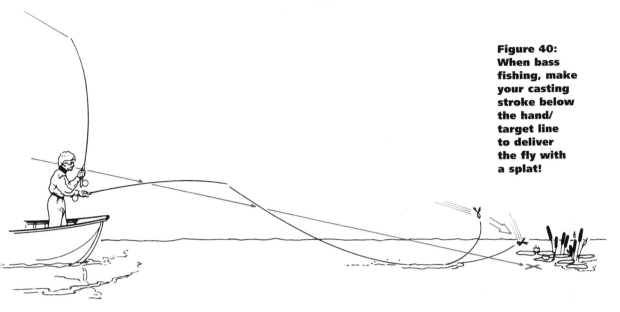

Figure 40: When bass fishing, make your casting stroke below the hand/ target line to deliver the fly with a splat!

from the water as described above for weighted nymphs. Be sure to allow the backcast to unroll fully.

Because bass aren't as spooky as cold-water species, the forward cast need not unroll completely above the water to land gently, but can first touch down 5 or 10 feet off the tip and unroll *on* the surface, presenting the fly with a *splat!*

Use a wide loop by power-snapping smoothly through the whole stroke, and incline the thumb pad's path to end below the hand/target line.

Bonefish, Permit, Tarpon

Figure 41: Casting to moving targets.

Moving fish must be intercepted. Accuracy depends on aiming at an imaginary moving target. Feed your inner calculator the necessary factors: speed

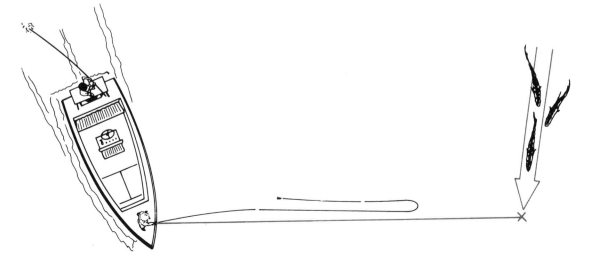

and direction of the moving fish, distance from you, and the effect of any wind. You'll be shooting line, so line-hand control to stop the cast where and when your eyes tell you is the final touch for accuracy.

Wind

Wind affects all casting. Before you begin your pickup, think about how the wind will affect the unrolling fly line: Where must the line travel to avoid colliding with your body? Think next about accuracy: Will the wind move the leader and fly to the right or to the left of the target? What is the best possible *angle* on which to place the power snap to counter the wind's effect?

HEAD-ON WIND

Factors:

> The cast will be blown back at you.
> Your strength is at its peak in a forward chopping motion.
> There is a cushion of calm air just above the water.

Figure 42: The low-angle option when casting in headwind.

CUSHION OF CALM AIR

For an overhead cast, stop your backcast at 12 o'clock; the wind will straighten it. Now *crouch*, presenting your forward cast with extra strength close to the water. Cast slightly below the hand/target line to unroll *on* the water.

Another option is to use an off-vertical or even a horizontal cast.

BACK WIND

Factors:

> The backcast will not be able to unroll.
> If you wait too long, you'll get hit with the line.

Use extra strength on the backcast; as soon as you complete the power snap, start the forward stroke. No waiting for the line to unroll, no drifting backward.

WIND FROM YOUR RIGHT

Factor:

You need to make the backcast pickup from the windward side, but you'll get hit on the forward cast.

Make the backcast with a little more speed, then, during drift time, tip the rod to a backhand position and make the forward cast on the leeward side. Back on the right; forward on the left. Depending on the angle from which the line must be lifted, you can also make both back and forward strokes in the backhand position (over your left shoulder). For either method, aim the loop to unroll the fly close to the water and perhaps a bit to the right of the target to compensate for the wind.

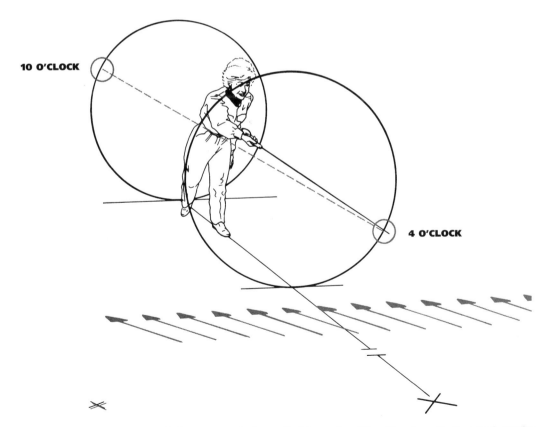

10 O'CLOCK

4 O'CLOCK

Figure 43: Left-front quartering wind is met with a (forehand) diagonal stroke.

WIND FROM YOUR LEFT

Factor:

The wind may blow your leader to the right.

Use a plane lower than vertical and aim a little left of the target.

QUARTERING WINDS

Left front quarter; right front quarter: You can compensate for these winds in either of two ways. Make the casting stroke *with* the wind, or *against* it; the wind's intensity will be the determining factor. With either choice, you'll want to position the rod to make the power snap on a *diagonal*, high to low across the face of the wind, from one side of the target or the other. Count on the wind to move the line toward the target but the diagonal will make the leader unroll close to the water—to be under the wind.

Imagine standing on a clock face, with your back to it and your feet at 6 and head at 12 o'clock. The diagonal path of your stroke will be 10 to 4 (forehand) or 2 to 8 (backhand) depending on whether you are going with the wind or against it (see figure 43).

Left rear quarter: Aim a little left of the target.

Right rear quarter: Cast backhand and aim a little right of the target.

CHAPTER 11

Indoor and Outdoor Practice

Casting with accuracy requires training the hand, forearm, and upper arm muscles to acquire strength and efficiency, but the core is eye/hand/target coordination. And that is a state of mind.

These are the principles you want to practice and make second nature: determining a hand/target line; beginning the power snap at roughly 90 degrees from the target on that line; ending the power snap at no less than 45 degrees from the target on that line.

Improving your casting can be a slow process or an accelerated one. The slow way is to practice occasionally and only outdoors, which may be very time consuming if you have to drive to a suitable area. The fast way is to practice indoors for short periods but very often, and outdoors whenever you can.

It's your hand and arm that direct and impulse the fly rod, and they're always with you. So to speed up your progress, hold any kind of a shaft in your hand—a pen, a cooking spoon, a table knife—and practice the motions and mechanics of the casting stroke and accuracy, wherever you are and whenever you want. Even using your indicator thumb without a rod will work. When you need a mental break from *anything*, think about the accuracy principles; this will improve your eye/hand/target coordination. It's that easy, but it's a state of mind. You have to commit to it.

Lee had an idea for an indoor practice rod that developed into a product called the Fly-O, a 3-foot rod with yarn for line (available from Royal Wulff Products in Livingston Manor, NY 12758). The yarn line doesn't shoot through the guides, but you can add length by pulling more of it outside the rod tip as you progress. With a 1:4 ratio of yarn to fly line (5 feet of yarn outside of the rod tip equals a 20-foot cast), this little rod can do wonders for serious casters.

The Fly-O is always ready; you can practice accuracy in your living room or office, choosing targets at different levels and distances to challenge yourself. The yarn's bulkiness makes its movement easy to follow. The results of your efforts are instantly apparent in the trajectory of the loop.

An exercise I call **picking leaves** will define the accuracy principles, using a Fly-O indoors or a rod and line outdoors. Once you understand the relationship of the rod arc to the target you can reinforce it any time of the day or night, with thumb in hand.

Ideally, the target area should be a bank of bushes as high as your head, but could be an automobile, a fence, or an area on a building. The goal is to aim at, and touch with your yarn fly, individual "leaves" in all of the planes—from horizontal on the right to nearly horizontal on the left, as described in chapter 6.

This is a *power-snap* exercise. Use 10 feet of line outside the rod tip, in addition to a 7½- to 9-foot leader and a yarn fly. With this line length, a power snap is sufficient to produce perfect loops. Position yourself far enough away so that the line, leader, and fly must fully unroll to touch a leaf.

Figure 44: Picking Leaves: Begin power snap at 90 degrees from the target leaf. End the power snap no more than 45 degrees later.

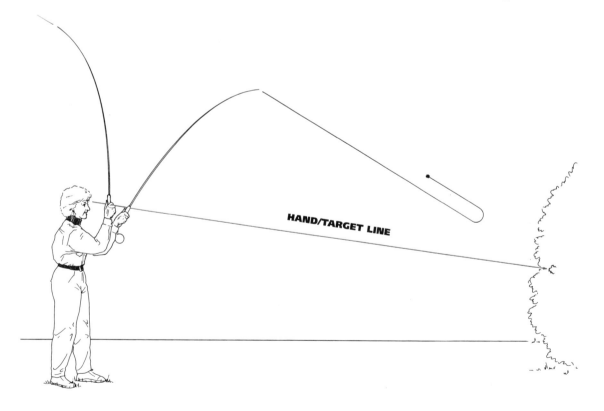

HAND/TARGET LINE

Pick out a leaf at eye level, and begin at the between-the-eyes rod position. With this short line, your backcast power snap must end 90 degrees from the target leaf, on the hand/target line, and the forward power snap must create an arc of no more than 45 degrees in the movement of the rod shaft toward the target. This 45-degree rod arc will produce an unrolling loop with no slack or bellying on a direct line to the target leaf.

You must *see* the loop and judge it on each forward cast. If there is any slack or if the loop doesn't unroll directly to the leaf, your power snap is too long.

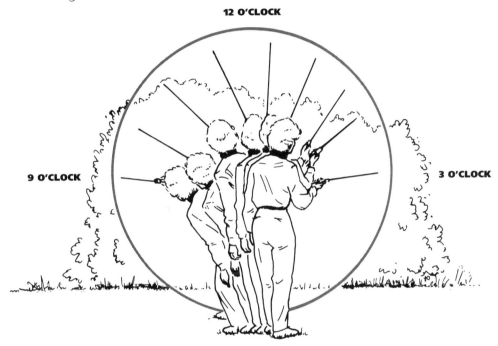

**Figure 45:
A good angler
can present a
fly accurately
at any angle
between 9 and
3 o'clock.**

Now change your angle. Slide into it gradually by casting in each plane (use the clock face) from 12 to 3 and then 12 to 9, staying with each until you have perfected the power-snap stroke. For the next step, as you leave one plane, make your backcast *opposite* the upcoming forward cast. For example, after casting between your eyes at 12 o'clock, make the next backcast lower, 90 degrees from 1 o'clock, then 90 degrees from 2 o'clock, and so on.

When you change from forehand to backhand or vice versa, you will need to reposition between power snaps, while the line is unrolling (*drift* time). This repositioning will always finish with the rod shaft in place at 90 degrees from the coming forward power snap.

When you have mastered the concept of where the power snap must be positioned to deliver the fly accurately, add another 10 or 15 feet of line, move farther away from the bush to accommodate the added length, and repeat the exercise, adding a *loading move* and *follow-through/drift* to your stroke. No matter where your arm moves between power snaps, position the rod shaft at roughly 90 degrees to the target before the forward snap.

With your rod and line, look for other outdoor challenges: Present the fly through a partially opened door, through an open car window, down an alley. Use anything out there, but know onto which particular inch you want to put your fly. You *will* get better and better and better at accuracy.

CHAPTER 12

Strengthening Your Casting Muscles

In the 1990s, an attention to physical fitness has changed the lifestyles of millions of people. Ordinary folks devote precious time to exercise as if preparing for Olympic competition! Not surprisingly, exercises specifically targeting the casting muscles are hard to find.

The late, great Charles Ritz, in his *Fly Fisher's Life* (1965), suggested simple weightlifting exercises using a wine bottle, empty at first, then gradually filled with sand, to dramatically improve muscle tone.

In a 1983 issue of *Fly Rod & Reel*, Glenn Law addressed the subject in an article titled "Pumping Graphite." I thought it good enough to save, and when I did my own research on the subject, it became obvious that I was reinventing the wheel. I give you Glenn's pertinent material, with only some changes in casting vocabulary to match the rest of this book.

But first some instructions: With barbells and sets of repetitions, your casting muscles can reach peak performance levels in weeks. For beginners, a woman should start training with a 1-pound weight; a man with a 3-pound weight. Begin with one set of fifteen reps (repetitions); gradually increase to a maximum of three sets of fifteen reps with whatever weight is comfortable.

And now in Glenn Law's words:

> The following selection of exercises conditions specific casting-related muscle groups. It was compiled by analyzing fly-casting requirements, and then drawing upon published exercise schedules recommended for a variety of other

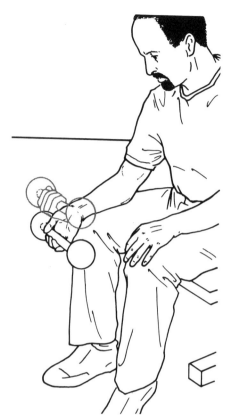

Figure 46: Palm-up wrist curl

sports, principally golf, racquetball, and throwing sports that utilize the same musculature as fly casting.

Wrist curls: This is a set of three variations on one exercise that conditions all the muscles of the forearm, wrist, hand, and fingers. The function of the forearm in casting is a complex interaction of all these muscles and joints and extremities, and conditioning them is perhaps the most beneficial preparation the fly caster can make, short of learning to tie good leader knots.

The first variation is the "palm-up" wrist curl. This is done sitting down with the forearm lying on the leg, and the hand holding the weight extending unsupported beyond the knee. Bending only at the wrist, the weight is raised as far as possible, then lowered slowly. At the lowest point, the fingers are extended and the weight is allowed to roll down the fingers. Be careful not to drop the weight at this point. Lift it back into the hand with the fingers, and this completes one repetition. This exercise strengthens the flexors, the muscles on the inside of the forearm, which are used in lifting line off the water and making the backcast power snap, and are important in developing line speed and lift behind the caster. Allowing the weight to roll down the fingers works wonders on the grip.

The second variation on the wrist curl is the "palm-down" version. It's performed the same way except the hand is reversed on the dumb-

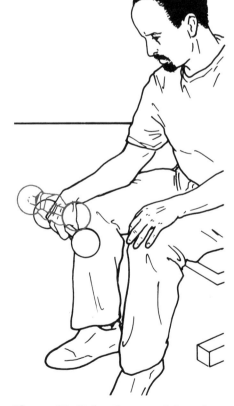

Figure 47: Palm-down wrist curl

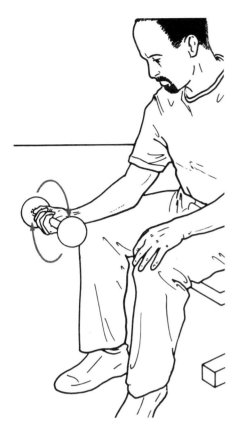

Figure 48: Wrist rotation

bell. This variation is more difficult than the first and may require less weight or fewer repetitions. The "palm-down" strengthens the muscles on the outside of the forearm (brachio radialis). These are the workhorses of the forearm and come into play in all phases of casting, especially on the forward-cast power snap. The strength of these muscles affects line control, loop formation, and a controlled presentation. Consequently, these muscles are responsible for both long-line effectiveness and short-line control and delicacy.

The third variation on the wrist curl is a rotational exercise. The wrist is held extended horizontally, and the weight is turned alternately to the left and the right. This strengthens the muscles of the wrist as well as the two large muscle groups of the forearm, and ties the forearm into a well-conditioned unit, aiding in a smooth and accurate transmission of power through all phases of casting.

Triceps curls: Also known as French Curls, this can be done with a single dumbbell (see figure 49) or with a pair of dumbbells exercising the arms separately. Sitting or standing, hold the weight overhead, then lower it behind your head by bending at the elbow only, and raise it again. This exercise isolates and conditions the triceps, the large muscle on the back of the upper arm. The triceps is the primary throwing muscle and performs nearly all of the upper-arm work in the forward cast. It

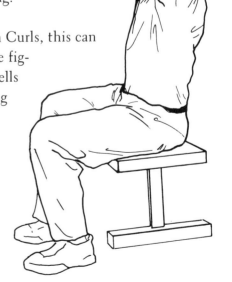

Figure 49: Triceps or French curl

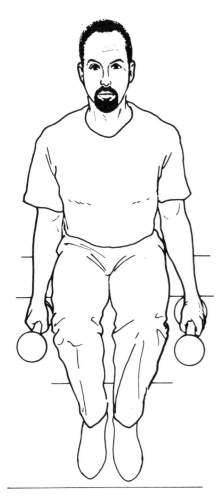

Figure 50: Biceps curl

provides a foundation for the actions of the forearm as well. Strong throwing muscles simply make casting less work. Well-conditioned triceps are especially helpful when casting in the wind, casting an especially bulky fly, or extending a cast.

Biceps curls: This exercise can also be done standing or sitting. The weight is held down at the side, then raised by bending at the elbow only, and lowered again slowly. This exercise works the biceps and brachialis muscles on the front of the upper arm. They perform the same function as the triceps but in reverse. (Muscles only contract; once contracted, another, opposing muscle must contract in turn to extend the first muscle.) The biceps are responsible for lifting line off the water and for strength to end the backcast power snap. The biceps also regulate elbow flex and affect forearm action and control through all phases of the cast.

Bent-over rowing: Bending over at the waist, let the weights hang straight down, then raise them to chest level, and lower them slowly. This exercise can also be done one arm at a time, adding a rolling motion of the torso at the top of the lift. Bent-over rows work two large muscle groups: the deltoids, the round muscles of the shoulders, and the latissimus, the broad sheet of muscle on the back. The deltoids support the arm through the full range of casting motions and are an important basis for all casting phases. If you've ever experienced a sore arm from casting, chances are the deltoids were the cause. As the shoulder is a primary pivot in fly casting, well-toned "delts" are essential for comfort and easy movement.

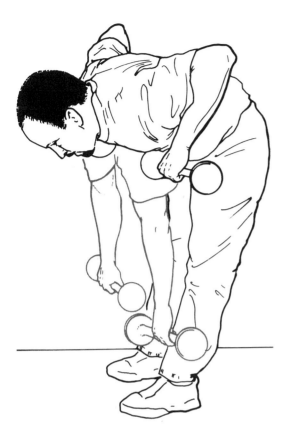

Perhaps the greatest benefit of this exercise is the strengthening of the back against injury and fatigue. The latissimus muscles are the cornerstone of all arm movement. When this exercise is done one arm at a time, the twisting movement at the top of the lift approximates the rocking motion of casting, aiding your flex and rhythm.

This completes a basic tour of the primary casting muscles. It is by no means a complete inventory of upper body fitness, but it covers all the most important functions the muscles perform in fly casting.

Thank you, Glenn.

I might add one more exercise: **Ulnar deviation**, to strengthen the muscles that control the motion of the

Figure 51: Bent-over rowing

wrist between bent down and straight.

Stand with your hands at your sides, each holding onto the end of a weighted bar (or the dumbbell), and bend the wrists laterally. Return slowly to the starting position.

There are products by the dozen that have been developed for strengthening hands, such as gripmaster. However, Ron Miller, strength coach of the Florida Marlins, ended a discussion of weight exercises with the suggestion that the "primitive" exercise of the hands' kneading action in a bucket of rice is still one of the very best.

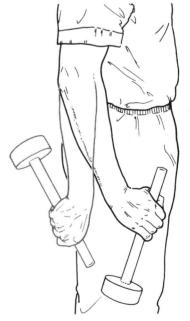

Figure 52: Ulnar deviation

Checklist

You now have a base from which to work the elements of accuracy, using the thumbnail and thumb pad indicators. The casts that make you operational have been covered, along with the horizontal-on-the-grass technique for "slow motion" analysis. Casting at all angles between horizontal on the left and horizontal on the right, and connecting the change of plane with the drift move, will solve 90 percent of your presentation problems. You should now know how to hover a fly for pinpoint accuracy when dry-fly fishing for trout.

Discipline is a shortcut to becoming accomplished at a sport. Refine your casting movements with this checklist:

➡ Remember that *power* is best applied *close to your body*, no matter how long the overall stroke may be.

➡ Keep your *elbow forward of your shoulder* through the power snap on every backcast, no matter what the angle or length of the stroke.

➡ Keep your *casting arm bent* through the forward power snap; it's only on the follow-through move that your arm even approaches straightening.

➡ Rely on the *strength of your hand and forearm*, not on your upper arm. Hand strength will control the narrowness of your loops and allow the subtlety of hovering a fly. Remember the screen door handle.

➡ *Short lines* have *high backcasts* with your thumbnail at forehead level; *long lines* have *lower backcasts* with your thumbnail just above your shoulder, about even with your chin.

➡ Horizontal casts are best made *no lower than elbow height* to maintain control during the power snap.

➡ Start with your *rod tip an inch or two above the water* to best effect the loading of the rod and the fitting in of the stroke elements in the space you have.

➡ Think ahead: Know where to *aim your backcast* to facilitate a change of direction or angle. Do all maneuvering *before* the forward-cast power snap.

We are not robots; no matter how much time we spend casting, or understanding the mechanics, we make mistakes. This is proved to me every time I fish. Still, if something goes wrong I know what it is and work to correct it on the next cast. When the pressure is on to be accurate, or to make my longest casts with a minimum number of strokes, cast after cast, I must think about what I am doing through the *entire* casting sequence. There is no taking for granted that a cast will be perfect. What I do take for granted is that if I look at a target area and push my thumb pad to it, power-snapping at what looks like the 90-degree mark, the fly should go there.

Creating a loop with a perfect trajectory results from the angle and length of the power snap. You will develop a sixth sense about this relationship. As the 90-degree-on-the-hand/target-line technique becomes second nature to you, you will be able to create a loop trajectory off the tip of the rod to suit your needs exactly—visualizing it, rather than thinking about how to do it.

This is what I wish for you.